Oh, My Child

Oh, My Child

The Cry
of Rachel Today

R . L . M c G e e

authorHOUSE®

AuthorHouse™ LLC
1663 Liberty Drive
Bloomington, IN 47403
www.authorhouse.com
Phone: 1-800-839-8640

Published by AuthorHouse   05/16/2014

ISBN: 978-1-4969-0967-1 (sc)
ISBN: 978-1-4969-0966-4 (e)

Contents

Introduction

This is a story based on the lives of real people, who never knew . . . The question still remains in their mind; "Who knew" . . . What made them snap?

Prologue

Live your life, but learn a lesson that comes with living. While you can breathe, you should hope. While you hope, you should expect to keep breathing. One doesn't work well without the other. We take charge of our lives to some extent, when we work these two "sidekicks" together. Never give up on seeking a spiritually rich life. Reach for the greatest relationship in the world. Of course, I mean reach for a relationship beyond humanity. Remember . . . "man will fail you", but there is one, beyond man, who never will fail you. He just continues to write new lesson plans for us until we reach a higher ground. Emotions run very high in many segments of my book. Please prepare yourself to laugh, cry, feel weary for some of the characters, cry for them and get angry about some of the situations. You will need to have, by your side a few things. Those things are: Your cell phone; because you will want to tell someone about what you are reading right away, a cool drink, a snack, and a box of tissue to wipe away your tears of laughter and your tears of sadness.

You may see someone that closely favors one or more of the characters depicted in this book. I have heard many say that they have seen themselves in this dynamic piece of work. You will enjoy this book because it is about real people and today's living experiences . . . you'll see.

<u>Acknowledgement</u>

I know, that there are broken homes all over the world and my heart truly goes out to those of you who are trapped in that hell. I know that there are women being abused and killed by the second and I am sorry that people don't have compassion for life the way they should. I know that there are children shut up in homes who are afraid to tell someone that they are being raped and misused. This is the one thing that I truly HATE!!! Leave our children alone! Women . . . "you better bash mister in the head and ask for forgiveness later" (that quote comes from and is accredited to the movie, "The color purple" (it is not my quote, but it is my feelings) To the men; God created you to look strong and not weak, to provide for others, to be a giver of life and not a taker. He gave you charge of naming living creatures, including Eve. He gave you power to tread over serpents . . . why on earth would you be willing to trade that power for a weaker stature? Hold your position by doing what you are created to do. Man, stand up and be the man that the Almighty God has ordained **_YOU_** to be; strong, compassionate and courageous! If you all read this poem, it will get you ready for the emotions within this story:

<u>Oxygen Tears</u>

Now we hear about the fate of an innocent woman,
who thought she was safe in a strange man's hands
Who heard her struggling? Oh, no one did!
She had to be quiet, for the sake of her kids

In his hands, she was as scared as could be
Every night she thought, "Will it be him or me?"
The odds were against her; she had many fears. She
cried, but no one saw her hot oxygen tears

We didn't know just how this would end
This was a message to all of her friends
"We don't know our final day or the hour"
"We do know that we depend on God's power"

On their faces was oxygen, big oxygen tears
The groans of their voices was echoing in our ears
She won't break down, no! He won't see her cry No,
she won't let him see wet tears in her eyes

Scene I
The Devil's play ground—the mind

Belinda, the receptionist is close to tears at her desk.
She is the person who works for Dr. Gilroy, the
psychologist in the hospital. She is on the telephone
attempting to calm a patient who is frantic. She can
feel his energy flowing in through the telephone. The
therapy room has chairs of different colors and styles
spread around the room. Dr. Gilroy enters the office
for a discharge review of patients.

>   (Belinda is talking to Leroy, a patient's son)

Belinda
You are going to have to get control of your father.

>   (Dr. Gilroy She sees Belinda's frustration and
>   sits in a chair across from Belinda)

Leroy
Now, how am I going to do that? This full grown
man is hopping on one leg, going around in circles
screaming "quack, quack, I'm a pink Cadillac. (In
the background you hear someone shouting, "Quack,
quack three times)

Belinda
If you can't control him, Leroy, you'll have to get him
down her for an exam.

Leroy
Can't y'all send one of them patty wagons to get him?
I am scared of this joker . . . What if he gets in the car

with me and thinks he is a stunt man or something and jumps out of the door. Oh, Lord! Please help me

(He's almost crying now)

Belinda:
Leroy I need you to call 911 and get him to the hospital right away. The staff will be waiting for your arrival.

Leroy
Yeah, that's what I will do. They have restraints in the ambulance and they are trained to do this kind of thing. Thank you, Jesus. I will call you when we get to the emergency room drive way.

Dr. Gilroy
Are you alright Belinda?

Belinda
I am fine Doctor. This is routine.

Dr. Gilroy
O.K, you are good at your job, Belinda

Belinda
Doctor, that's what your mouth says. How about saying it with a raise?

(Belinda stared at her briefly)

Dr. Gilroy
Don't I have a group discharge session this morning?

<u>Belinda</u>:
Yes, doctor. They are on the way

<u>Dr. Gilroy</u>
And is their Pastor confirmed to be here? You know he is coming to reconnect with them and invite them to the church today.

<u>Belinda</u>
I thought that Church was the final field day in the program.

<u>Dr. Gilroy</u>
It is, but, we don't want it to seem like we are forcing religion on them.

(Pastor Wright enters the room)

<u>Dr. Gilroy</u>
Good morning, Pastor Wright. Please come with me.

(Dr. Gilroy and Pastor Wright went into the lab room)

<u>Dr. Gilroy</u>
Will you also transport them to the church with you?

<u>Pastor Wright</u>
Yes, Dr. Gilroy, I will take all those that will come with me. You know that the Lord gave us choice.

(Everyone enters the back door, one at a time and stops briefly at Belinda's desk to sign in)

(They are all sitting and suddenly they began talking)

Ruby
Who knew . . . that one day I would look at my daughter with sorrow and fears? Who knew that she would run away from me, leaving me home with nothing to remember her by, except tears and fears? I didn't consent to her leaving, she ran away from me! Now she returns beaten by poverty, loneliness and abuse? Who knew?

Butch
Who knew that my innocent and sweet son would follow the wrong crowd and desert his real dreams of becoming a successful powerhouse in business? He once counted his pennies from selling his bubble gum from his gum ball machine and he was killed counting dollars from selling white balls of crack from a pack. I hurt so badly, man. I drink to keep my head straight. Who knew?

Mary
Who knew that my baby girl, who continued to proclaim that she wanted to become a nun since she was a young child, would find herself locked up in a room with a stranger who was psychotic? I never thought that I would buckle down to my knees and be reminded of the unforgettable, excruciating and uncontrollable labor pain of her birth. I felt it all over again when she told me of her horrible experience with this stranger. Who Knew?

Jessie

I was so happy and proud to be his son. He was glad
to have me as a son. Something went wrong, but God
knows best. I remember playing with him when I
took my first step. He tossed me in the air and man
he laughed and I laughed, he laughed and I laughed.
I was laughing because I could feel gravity bringing
me down with every bit of laughter that we shared.
He left me and my mother, then, it became the weight
of our so-called environment that brought me down.
When I was young, I laughed and then I cried. Now,
no weapon formed against me shall be able to prosper.

Willie

When she needed understanding, I was not there. When
she needed strong arms to protect her, I was not there.
So, what happened? How is it that when she closed
her eyes and took a deep breath to prepare her for her
adolescence, I slipped into her world, stole her strong
will and kidnapped her innocence? She was not ready
for this type of experience. She still played with dolls.
My heart still breaks into little pieces. Yes, she told her
mom about her experience. I was so sick with shame
that I felt like killing someone . . . especially when she
cried. Yes, she cried, her mother cried and I cried. They
cried and I cried. We cried, we cried and we cried. I
wanted to kill myself, but they would not let me.

Alice

So, what's the deal? Is this for real? There's something
missing from this recipe called Love. All over the world,
we see the same thing over and over again. People say
they love each other, but something is awfully wrong. If
we can't love each other, how can we love God?

Belinda

Good morning! We will be with you soon. Have a seat please.

> (They all remained in their chairs)
> (Dr. Gilroy entered the room)

<u>Dr. Gilroy</u>

Good morning, everyone, follow me please.

> (They all went into the lab room)

The walls are all white and there are no pictures on the walls. All of the chairs in this room are black. She prefers not to assist their imaginations, so that she can bring about true emotions.

<u>Everyone</u>

Good morning doctor

<u>Dr. Gilroy</u>

Good Morning. Okay everyone, you all know each other from the community. Bring your chairs together to form a half circle so we can complete your discharge review.

> (Everyone got a chair from the wall)
> (Place them in a half circle)
> (Everyone sits, including the counselor)

After this session, you will be placed on an out-patient basis only. This final exercise will, hopefully, bring closure to the issues that bothered you. Let me say that I am hopeful for your successful return to the community. Your last exercise is to attend a church today. Right now, you will stand one at a time and tell us what brought you here to mental counseling in the first place. I need to evaluate you to see if you have faced your demons. After this intervention your Pastor Wright is here to speak to you concerning church.

(Pastor stands and smiles)

Pastor
Good morning everyone. It is good to see you

(Pastor sits back down in his seat)

Dr. Gilroy
Perhaps at a later time you all will come together to express your experiences and support each other. Let's begin now with our final exercise. Alice, would you please stand and begin? Each of you will begin and end you story with the words, "Who knew".

After you tell your initial story, I want each of you to exchange deeper feelings about your experience in a conversation with the others.

(Alice sits upright with her arms folded)

Dr. Gilroy
Would you stand, please, Alice? What's on your mind, Alice? Alice, is there anything you would like to say or ask anyone in the room? Alice. Are you okay.

(Dr. Gilroy looked concerned)

Alice
I'm okay. Um, thank you. I have nothing to add.

Dr. Gilroy
Now Alice, we have been over this a couple times. No one person is an island.

> (Alice nods yes)
> (As the counselor is about to continue her conversation)
> (Alice interrupts the conversation)
> (Suddenly the scene got very dramatic)
> (Alice quickly stands to her feet)

Alice
Why do we have children?

> (Mary walks to the end of the row behind her and turns her back to the audience briefly)
> (Mary turns back to the audience but continues to stand)
> (Butch remains seated)

Butch
Don't people know?

> (Mary stands and turns to look at Butch, then sits down)
> (Alice scoots to the edge of her seat and leans out, looks at the counselor)

<u>Alice</u>
Babies are not just live toys . . .

     (Jessie remains seated)

<u>Jessie</u>
They play with them or look, at them only to admire them but teach them nothing!

     (Willie walks from woman to woman flirting
     and touching them)

<u>Willie</u>
May I share my theory about living stones called humans? Spirits are poured into each human before birth.

     (Willie returns to his seat but, remains standing
     with his hand in his pocket for 5 seconds)
     (Willie sits down)

<u>Mary</u>
     (Chuckling)

Every living human is created from the interaction between a man's and a woman's body.

     (Butch stands and demonstrates where his
     eyes, ears, and mouth are as he speaks)

<u>Butch</u>
I believe one thing, in order for us all to have two eyes, two ears, one mouth and one nose . . . all in the basic same place on a normal face, had to be a planned design.

(Butch sits)
(Mary walks to the front)

Mary

(She walks behind her chair)
(She points to the sky with her pointing finger)

This has to be a finger print of a power so great that it cannot be duplicated without using some part of the creation that was already made.

(She puts her finger down and puts her right hand on her hip)
(The doctor grabs her arm gently to take her back to her seat)
(Alice stands up, walks to the front, using hand and open arm expressions)

Alice

For example, cloning cannot be done unless some part of the original design is used. It simply cannot be duplicated.

(Belinda goes to get Alice and take her back to her seat)
(Mary stands up with her hands to her side)
(Mary is crying now)

Mary

Parents are supposed to keep, nurture, feed, protect and guard their children to make them ready to minister for God.

(Dr. Gilroy helps Mary to sit down)

(Alice remains in her seat)

Alice
You are free to believe

(Willie remains in his seat shaking his head)

Willie
Or disbelieve this.

Alice
I cried, but, no one saw the wet tears in my eyes.

(Alice is shaking her head and wringing her hands).
(Helen stands, moves into Willie's face and yells at Willie)

Helen
You think that I was a bad friend. She left me. I was a good friend.

(Willie stands up to Helen)
(Yelling back)

Willie
You were a lover. Yeah I said it.

(Belinda helps Helen back to her seat)
(Willie pauses briefly-for 5 seconds)

I don't really think that. I think that I was a bad father. Somebody should have taught me. My heart breaks every day.

(Willie looks at Helen and turns to the others)
(He hunches his shoulders and sits down)
(Helen rises, walking to the counselor,
screaming with tears flowing)
(Mary is looking directly at the counselor now)

Mary

She was beaten every day and I didn't know it . . . and
he was a drug dealer! She was in danger every day!
Oh, my baby.

(Mary is buckled down with her arms
hugging her stomach)
(The Dr. Gilroy helps her sit down)
(Butch turns and walks to the front with his
head down)

Butch

I am depressed now and I need my drink to keep me
stable. I just can't get a foot hold on life. I wasn't there to
guide him. The military was my God. Lord, forgive me.

PLEASE! (Yelling)

(Mary stands again)

Mary

My baby, oh, my baby. I know that I should have
protected her. I didn't take her to church because my
drug kept saying that there is no hope there. Well, the
hope is there. I did it wrong?

(Dr. Gilroy helps her sit down again)
(Willie loses it)

Willie

>   (Yelling)

Church! My entire family is a big mess!!! We never
went to church.

>   (Willie quickly walks across the table)
>   (Willie returns, but he is walking in circles)
>   (The Dr. Gilroy grabs Willie by the hand and
>   sits him in his seat)

Jessie

Shut up! Shut up! I mean all of you.

>   (Jessie gets down on his knees and on the
>   floor)
>   (He puts his hands over his ears)

These are the things that happen when we are selves
are bad.

>   (Jessie stays there, with his ears covered,
>   until the Dr. Gilroy gets him up)
>   (Dr. Gilroy helps Jessie up and leads him to
>   his seat)
>   (Helen gets up, faces the counselor and
>   slowly walks backward)
>   (Helen accidently bumps into Butch)
>   (Butch yells)
>   (Belinda hears the noise and come into the
>   lab to help Dr. Gilroy)

Butch

Get off me!!! Don't touch me!

> (Dr. Gilroy gets Ruby back to her seat)
> (Belinda gets Butch back into his seat)
> (Helen is screaming and crying on her way to her seat)

Helen

Oh, what a vicious web we have woven. I hate this! I hate this!

> (Willie stands in front of his seat)

Willie

Hey, wait! We need to go to church real bad.

> (Everyone gets quiet and all we hear is sniffling and groans from all)

We need Jesus, but I have to go back to my restaurant today. Will you all pray for me?

> (Willie opens his arms with the question)
> (Everyone remains seated)

Jessie

Yeah, Jesus will help us. Let's go back to the old land mark. That's all I Want right now. Willie, we will pray for you, brother.

Ruby

O-o-o, I don't know. I am not sure.

Mary
She's right. I mean, won't the people there judge us.

Pastor Wright
They won't. If anyone does, I'll be the first to deal with them.

(The group looks at each other and they nod yes.)

Jessie
Doctor, would you please come with us as well?

Dr. Gilroy
No, Jessie. This is the end of the road for me. I must keep our relationship professional

Butch
There is an incredible cafe next to the church.

Dr. Gilroy
I do enjoy a good meal.

(She looks at her belly and pats her stomach)

I will go, but this one time only. We will consider this as our farewell gathering, O.K.?

Butch
I understand.

Ruby
I agree with that.

Dr. Gilroy
(Sophisticated tone)

Go ahead and put your chairs back on the wall and then gather around me. I have something for you. I wrote a poem for you all to hear and remember as you go on with your lives. Listen.

Our minds and our hearts challenge each other.
ISMS come in bunches as you will discover.
Strength is a flower that smells like a daisy.
ISMS are your events that will drive us crazy.
Speak positive of yourself, demand it from others. Do not forget to raise and look under their covers, not just the brothers, but sisters and bad lovers.
Count on who loves you; God and your mother

You are creature that God has made, who; bundle, bunch and cradle your babe
Clip the wings of your unforgettable past,
Cut your loss, let go and toss it like trash . . .
Because, that is what it is. It's your past trash

Now, I hope that none of you return here again. Keep your heads up. I will meet you at your church. Bye now

      (They all leave)
      (Dr. Gilroy leaves with the Pastor)

Pastor
      (Pastor Wright stands up)

Well, everyone, it looks like you will be just fine, praise the Lord. Now, I would like you all to come on back to the church today. I have a van down stairs and I will be responsible to get you to church. Is that alright?

(They all nodded yes)

Scene II
In Church

The church is a small store front church which is quite old. It is red brick with a wooden heavy door. Inside was semi bright with one picture on the wall, a podium (It was made of wood), and absolutely no furniture, except the pastor's and the associate pastor's chairs.

(Pastor sits in the Pastor seat)
(Jessie sits in the associate Pastor's seat)

The church is filled with various people including the ones from the hospital. Leola, Helen and Alice is in front

Pastor Wright Amen.   (Yelling)

Congregation   (Loud voices shouting)
Amen.

(Pastor speaks in a normal tone)

Are you with me today, church? The message for today is that God will forgive us, no matter what we have done, if we ask him to.

(The Pastor pauses)

We are to keep.

ALL
Keep!

Pastor Wright Nurture!

Jessie
Uh Huh!

Pastor Wright   (Preaching rhythm)

Protect, feed and prepare our children in the ways
of God. We got to teach them how to repent quickly
when they fall into sin.

> (Pearl is raising her hand up and waving it)
> (Pearl takes her hand down)

Pearl   (Yelling)
Preach it Pastor Wright.

> (Pastor Wright looks at Pearl)

Pastor Wright
We are to guard them and pray with them that they
may be ready to minister for God. Amen? Let's turn
to James 5th chapter.

> (Pastor Wright turns a page of his Bible)

Turn to the 16th verse which tells us to confess our trespasses one to another, that we may be healed. It also tells us to be fervent in prayer . . .

>(We see Pearl and Jessie looking in their Bibles)
>Both lift their heads up and exchange glances)
>(Pearl clears her throat)
>(Leola looks at her)
>(Pearl waves her Bible at Leola, pointing to it, telling her to open her Bible)

Pearl
Open your Bible, girl

>(The other two ladies see this and open their Bible too)

Pastor Wright
For the effective fervent prayer of the righteous avails much. Somebody say amen!!

All
Amen!

Pastor Wright
Listen Church, Sister Pearl, our minister of music, she uh . . .

>(Pearl look directly at Pastor Wright)

Pastor Wright (con't)
She has been out of the church for some time now, going through some trials in her life . . .

(Pastor Wright pauses for a moment)
(He looks up to the roof, points up and looks at the congregation)

But, God!

<u>All</u>
But God!!!

<u>Pastor Wright</u>
I know that we all are glad to see her back with us. Amen?! Now, I don't mean to surprise you, Sister Alice, with my request.

(Alice has a smile on her face)
(Alice stands in place)

But, uh, ah Sister Pearl, would you bless us with a song of praise this morning?

(Pearl holds her bible in her chest and walks up to the front of the church)
(She stands on the right of Pastor Wright's pulpit)
(Pastor Wright moves away from the Pulpit and sits in his chair)
(Pearl faces the congregation)

<u>Pearl</u>
Hallelujah! God is good!

(In a stern tone)

Pastor . . . Saints.

(In a normal tone)

I have been gone from the church for a while because
of my affliction, but I'm still here. My friends left me,
but I am still here. The devil attacked me, but . . .

(Leola looks at Pearl and doesn't say
anything for a few seconds)
(Leola looks back at the congregation)

. . . I am still here. The doctors said it was over, but I
am still here.

(Voice cracks)
(Alice nudges Helen)

Alice
I wish she wasn't here. I wish she would disappear.

(Helen nudges Leola)

<u>Helen</u>
Be quiet, Leola. You are in God's house. Don't make
him strike you down in here.

<u>Pearl</u>
Some days I was so weak and all I could do was cry
and pray. (She is speaking in a whiny tone)

But, I am still here. I am going to calm down, you
all. I am going to sing this song because it is my
testimony. Yea though I walked through the valley
and the shadow of death, I did not fear any evil . . .
because the Lord held my hand and he walked with

me in my storm and he never left me alone. This is what I prayed every day, church.

> (Everyone is rejoicing, saying "Hallelujah, say it Sister or Amen")
> (Pearl sings the song "Walk with me Lord")

Walk with me Lord; walk with me, Walk with me Lord; walk with me, While, I'm on this tedious journey. I want Jesus to walk with me. Hold my hand Lord, please hold my hand Hold my hand Lord; hold my hand. While I'm on this tedious journey, I want Jesus to hold my hand. Be my friend, Lord. Be my friend. Be my friend, Lord. Be my friend. While I'm on this tedious journey, I want Jesus to be my friend.

> (Pearl stops singing and everyone claps and shouts)

<u>Leola</u>   (She is screaming)

Yes, sir! Yes, Lord!

<u>Helen</u>
Yes, Lord. Thank you Lord!

> (Pastor Wright is still clapping his hands for about 5 seconds longer than everyone else)

<u>Pastor Wright</u>
Thank God for that wonderful selection. Amen! Say Amen saints. He tried . . . but he couldn't stop her!

Friends left her and God became her closest friend.

>   (He is so excited now)

Woo!!! Hallelujah!

>   (He reduces the volume to a normal tone)

I am going to calm down myself, you all. Let's bow our heads and pray.

>   (The congregation and Pastor Wright bow their heads)

Lord, we ask you to be ever present in all that we do. We pray for peace and traveling mercy for each and every person that is traveling or those here about to leave this church.

>   (Pastor Wright raises his head up and looks all over the congregation)

Pastor Wright (con't)
Keep the enemy away and bind him in the name of Jesus. Lord, thank you for this day. Take care of us until we meet again. Amen. Now, one last announcement, we will meet at our regular spot in the "No-ISMS" Cafe next door to break bread together. Now let's all end church with the benediction. May the Lord watch between me and thee, while, we are absent one from the other in Jesus name. Amen.

>   (Everyone in the church raises one hand)
>   (Everyone sing "God be with you")

All

God be with you, God be with you . . . God be with you . . . until we met again. God be with you, God be with you . . . God be with you until we meet again.

>(Alice walks to the back door behind the pulpit)
>(Alice is waiting by the back door for Leola and Helen to join her)
>(Alice is waving at them to come)
>(Helen and Leola act like they don't see her)
>(She still feels a bit uncomfortable touching other people)
>(She doesn't want to bump into anyone by accident)
>(She finally leaves out the back door)

Scene III
Uncovered secrets in No—ISMS restaurant

>(Alice walked alone to the café and waits)
>(Leola and Helen enters in at the door)
>(All three ladies meet at the cafe door)
>(The ladies enter door)
>(The three of the take a seat in the waiting area)
>(Helen sits on the far end, then Leola, then Alice)

Helen

Hey Alice, I saw you at the back door

Leola

Are you okay? Anything we can help you with?

>(Alice continues to keep her cool)

<u>Alice</u>
I'm okay. Just felt a little weird. That's all.

<u>Leola</u>
You can tell us. Maybe we can help.

<u>Alice</u>
No. I'm good.

<u>Leola</u>
Sister, are you going to that big oldies concert next Saturday?

<u>Helen</u>
Alice, we never see you anywhere but church and Wednesday bible meetings.

<u>Alice</u>
And so, what does that mean?

<u>Leola</u>
Hold up girl. Do you mean don't want to talk about that or you don't want to talk to us?

<u>Alice</u>
      (Alice changes the subject)

I want to sit at a good table. This restaurant is very nice with an elegant setting.

      (Rene standing next to the cash register)
      (Rene is on the telephone)
      (Alice sees her hands are dry and she grabs for her hand sanitizer and lotion from her purse)

(She puts it on her hands and in the palm of
Leola and Helens hands)
(Rene sees Helen, Leola, and Alice)
(Rene calls out for the Willie and Taylor)

Rene

Oh, my goodness! It's that time already?

(Rene is yelling)

Willie! Taylor!

(Willie and Taylor rushes out of the kitchen
and approach Rene at the podium)

Your Sunday after church group is coming in loud and
crazy!
I hope the Lord calms them down. I am not in the
mood today.

(Willie and Taylor look real hard at the three
ladies)
(Willie and Taylor turn back to Rene)

Willie

Lord, help us today. Especially these three loud
women right over there.

(Taylor, Rene and Willie are in a huddle.)
(Willie looks and points his finger close
range at both Taylor and Rene)

Taylor, Rene. You all stand by.

(Taylor has an angry look on his face and stares at both of them.)
(Taylor then walks to the kitchen)
(Rene sees Leola, Helen, and Alice)
(Rene walks over to them at the waiting area)

Rene

Is it a party of three today ladies?

(Everyone remains silent for a few seconds)
(Leola looks at both of the women and then at Rene)

Leola

That's correct.

(Rene looks around and doesn't see an empty table.)
(She has a nervous look and then sees a clear table in the center of the café)

Rene

Follow me ladies?

(The women followed Rene to the table)
(While they are walking Rene looks at Leola)

How did you like church today?

Leola

It was great!

(Leola follows Rene and sits in the center of the table)

(More people start to arrive at the café)

Alice Sure was

> (Leola sits in the center seat, Alice sits on the right of the table and Helen is sitting on the left of the table)

Helen

And that's the truth! I am so ready to eat. I haven't eaten a thing since last night.

> (Helen picks up the menu and her eyes look all over the menu)

Leola

> (She is being sarcastically)

I doubt that . . . very much!

Alice

I don't know where she puts all of that food. She doesn't gain a pound.

> (Helen has a cheesy grin on her face)
> (She uses her feet to pull off her heels)

Boy! My feet are hurting from standing in church so long.

> (Alice uses one of her hands to massage her feet)

Helen

Don't touch your feet in here, girl! Here is the sanitizer, Alice. You should stop wearing those hooker heels to church.

> (Jokingly)

You knew we didn't have any furniture in the church when you put those shoes on.

> (Alice is taken back by Helen's remark and unable to keep her cool)

Alice   (Sarcastic)

I got these hooker heels from your momma.

> (Helen points her finger at Alice)

Helen   (She is upset)

What!?

> (Helen gets up from her chair and glares at Alice.)

You don't talk about my momma. Girl!

> (Alice waves her hand towards Helen.)

Alice

Oh calm down child, you started this mess.

> (Alice rolls her eyes at Helen for being too serious)

Helen

Yeah, but I didn't talk about your momma, did I?

> (Alice gets up from her seat.)
> (She is stiff and ready to take the argument further)
> (Leola gives both of them a glare)

Leola

You both are a hot mess. Be quiet, both of you.

> (Helen and Alice get quiet)
> (Everyone is silent for five seconds. (Leola notices the silence at the table and starts to talk)

Wow. Sister Alice sure did sing that song today, don't you think so?

Leola

She tore it up! Umph, umph, umph!!

Helen

Pastor Wright preached his heart out too, didn't he.

> (Everybody at the table nods)
> (Pearl enter the room)

Pearl

You know there are too many people trying to take care of others peoples business and they can't even take care of their own. Watch them start some junk.

> (Pearl stops mumbling)
> (Pearl then looks at Rene)

(Rene immediately led her from table to table
to sit)
(Pearl keeps shaking her head "No" at Rene)
(Rene leads Pearl to the Leola's table)

Rene

Sister Pearl, well, maybe you want to sit with your
church sisters?

(Pearl turns and stares at Rene)

Sister Pearl, do you want to sit with them?

(As Pearl and Rene get closer to Leola's table,
they hear the women's conversation)

Pearl

I don't want to sit with them heathen. I just don't want
to!!!!

(Pearl looks at Rene angrily and back at
Leola's table)
(Pearl and Rene turned around to go to the
back table near Leola)
(Leola and the other two women are whispering
and gesturing about Pearls nappy hair)

Leola

Did you hear that? If Sister Pearl comes to church one
more time with that row of naps in the back of her neck,

(She speaks in a joking tone)

I'm just going to lay hands on her head. Ms. Pearl is a hot mess.

> (Pearl walks toward Leola following Rene)

Pearl
I heard your big old mouth at the front door, Leola.

> (Leola has a shocked look)
> (The other women are silent)
> (Pearl steps to Leola and point at Leola)

Pearl
Thank God that I am not the woman that I was before God saved me or you would have a real problem.

> (Leola points at herself)

Leola
Who me?

> (Leola stands up and gets in Pearl's face)

Pearl
Yes . . . you, Ms. Leola with A.D.D.

> (Rene notices a problem and gets in front of Pearl to calm her down)
> (Pearl has a stern look on her face)
> (Rene puts both hands in the air to make a stop gesture)

Rene

Now, Sister Pearl, let's get you something to drink.
Would you like coffee or something else to drink?

> (Rene is rubbing Pearl's her arm and guiding
> her back to her seat to get her away from Leola)

Alright, come with me over here to this nice table.

> (Pearl jerks away from Rene)

Pearl

Excuse me!

> (Pearl has an angry look)

Do I look like an invalid to you? Will you let go of my
arm, please!!!?

> (Rene lets go of Pearl's arm)
> (Pearl continues to stare down at Leola)
> (Leola begins to get a tense look on her face)

Pearl

You all better keep my name out of your mouths . . .
Leola! You better check yourself . . . Hallelujah!

> (Willie and Taylor notice a problem at Leola's
> table)
> (Both of them swiftly walks over—but not too
> fast to attract attention to a tense situation)
> (All of people in the cafe are looking at them)

Rene

Ms. Pearl, you are wearing a nice looking dress today. Where did you get it?

> (Rene calms Pearl with fashion talk)
> (Pearl starts to calm down and sits at her seat)

Pearl

> (Shock and wide eyed)

I, uh, I uh . . . yeah . . .

> (Pearl speaks in a normal tone)

I got this from Sharon's boutique. It's a real nice little shop. You should see the hats that I found. You know I am on a fixed income, but I like to look nice too, just like those little Heathens over there.

Rene

Oh, alright, Sister Pearl. I'll be right back.

> (Pearl continues to look at Leola)
> (Rene goes to help another customer)
> (Willie approaches Pearl from stage left)
> (He smiles at Pearl)

Willie

Don't let those three women upset you today. You don't need them to steal your joy with their bitterness.

> (Willie's smile gets so big you can see his teeth)

Willie
You know better than that Ms. Pearl.

Pearl
I know it, Willie.

> (Rene walks back to the waiter's area and
> sees Taylor)

Rene
Taylor, would you help me? I have to get drink orders
for those women at that table.

> (Rene points to Taylor across Leola's table)
> (Taylor grabs the drinks and takes them to
> the women)
> (Rene is walking towards Pearl's table from
> up stage left)
> (Taylor waves at Rene and Rene leaves)
> (Pearl looking at Rene)

Pearl
Those women get on my last nerve. Hypocrites, plain
hypocrites!!!

> (Rene nods and goes back to the Leola's table)

Rene
Are you ladies ready to order yet?

> (Helen puts the menu down and looks at Rene)

Helen

Since you asked; coffee for me.

> (Helen looks at the two other women)
> (Both of them keep quiet)
> (She speaks with an irritated tone)

I mean for the three of us, OK.

> (The other two women nod their heads)

Rene

Alright, I'll be right back with your coffees.

> (Rene walks over to the kitchen area on stage left)
> (Rene is at the coffee machine and turns it on)
> (While the machine warns up she grabs cups)
> (Rene puts coffee in each of the cups)
> (Willie is leaning against the kitchen wall holding a picture in his hand)
> (Rene passes by with the coffee cups)
> Willie sees Rene coming his way and stops her)

Willie

Where is Taylor?

> (Rene is frustrated since the drinks are burning hot)
> (Taylor walks out of the restroom door and sits at the Table nearest to the restroom door)

Rene (Rene is irritated)
I don't know, Willie. Watching him is your job. That lazy
scoundrel . . . You won't find him, Good luck though.

> (Rene continues to walk past Willie. (Willie
> turns himself around and looks right at Taylor)

Willie
You are on my last nerve. Go to work Taylor.

Taylor
I am at work . . . man

> (Speaking under his breath in a sarcastic way)

I know you enjoy my company, Willie. My
personality is what keeps you going. You need me
around here.

> (Willie shakes his head and walks to chat
> with Pearl)

Willie
> (He is upset)

That little . . .

> (He speaks in a normal tone talking to himself)

Keep calm Willie. You were a kid once too.

> (Rene gets to the table and pulls out cup mats
> from her apron and puts the cup mats on
> Leola's table)

Helen

Yeah girl, you'd better hush up. Pearl is going to beat you up. You keep it up.

You know she will fight a man, don't you?

> (Rene sets the coffee cups on the coffee mats while the women continue talking).

She is saved, but she will fight a man. I heard about her past. She has a reputation of fighting men and beating them too.

Alice

Yeah, girl . . . You better hush and how you gone talk about sister Pearl's naps? Your head haven't been seen in ages without that big ole weave sitting on top of it.

What's that all about? You gone get yourself beat up. Wait a minute!!! Let me see what's under that bun.

> (Alice is reaching for Leola's hair).
> (Leola has a shocked look on her face).

Leola

Hold up, Ms. Alice. Leola checks her weave and talks back to Alice.

I know that you are not trying to play the dozens with me? That's dumb, you know me.

> (She speaks in a stern tone)

I don't play.

(Leola gives both Alice and Helen a firm stare)
(Both stop. Leola looks away from both women)
(Leola sips her coffee and savors its flavor)

Helen

Okay, now, you all know that Proverbs 11:13 says "A gossip betrays a confidence, but a trustworthy man keeps a secret" . . .

(Helen then points at Leola)

You talk too much, Leola.

Leola

Wait! Did I miss something? I look good with hair or without hair. (Leola pulls out a pocket mirror from her purse and looks at her hair). I can flip it Flop it.

(Leola moves her head back)
(Leola moves her head forward)

Or smack it clean. I know that I look good. So, pump your brakes Alice. PUMP . . . YO . . . BRAKES

Helen

This is not about you!

(Pastor Wright enters the restaurant and as he enters, he notices Pearl and greets her)

Pastor Wright

Hello sister Pearl!

Pearl
Hello Pastor

>   (Pearl gets up from her chair and gives Pastor
>   Wright a hand shake)
>   (Pastor Wright then looks around and sees
>   Leola) (He turns back to Pearl)

Pastor Wright
Sister Pearl. You were incredible. God gave you a gift.

Pearl
Thank you Pastor. He also gave me a good pastor.

>   (Pastor Wright walks further toward Leola,
>   Helen and Alice's table)

Pastor Wright
Is everything alright Sisters?

>   (Pastor Wright then looks around the café)
>   (Pearl doesn't say anything but stares at Leola)
>   (Pastor Wright feels tension from her and
>   notices the stare between Leola and Pearl)

Pastor Wright (Loud)
Good afternoon everyone.

>   (Everyone in the cafe looks at Pastor Wright
>   then makes a big deal over his entry by
>   watching his every move) (Pastor Wright
>   walks over to and stands in the back of
>   Leola's table)

Pastor Wright

Good afternoon ladies? Are you ladies on your good behavior this afternoon? Or am I going to have to minister to you in here today?

> (Pastor Wright looks at each one)

Cause I know the three of you. God is watching and I am always listening.

> (Pastor Wright then moves to the left end of the table)

Now, don't you all put me up in your little evil

> (Pastor clears his throat and continues to talk to the ladies)

God don't like ugly and you know I won't tolerate this non sense. Amen.

Alice, Leola and Helen Amen.

> (Pastor Wright looks at the three women)

Now what damage have you done in here?

Helen

No damage this time Pastor. (Helen glares at Leola) It's not that Leola wasn't trying. Leola, you better stop talking bad about people. What goes around comes around.

> (Leola has a look of shock and stands up from her chair)

Leola

Oh, you hush.

>   (Helen gets up from her chair) (Leola is
>   condescending)

Just shut up Helen . . .

Helen

>   (Yelling)

No!!!! You shut up before you get beat up!!! (Yelling)
My momma don't even tell me to shut up, you can say
hush up to me. But don't tell me to shut up.

>   (Everyone in the cafe tries to ignore the
>   argument at Leola's table)
>   (People are eyeballing Helen)
>   (Pastor Wright looks at the people at the
>   nearest table)

Pastor Wright

They are just a little passionate about the some things.

You all go on and enjoy your meals.

Leola

Oh, Girl . . . you be quiet. Loosen up your girdle.
You shoal have a lot of ISMS or Schisms but you try
to act like you don't. You women talk about me like
I'm some kind of broke down wagon or something. I
know it and you do too.

(As Leola talks Helen sits back down)
(Leola continues to stare at Helen)

Now, I am not one to gossip but I will bet if I was a
betting woman, you got some secrets or some ISMS.
Now you know that I am not ashamed of what I do.

> (Leola picks up her cup and takes a quick
> drink)

I don't much care what other people think about
Leola . . . Leola looks at both of Helen and Alice.
That's why we get along so well.

> (Leola makes a hand gesture pointing at all
> three of them)

It's the three of us, you know.

> (Leola rolls her eyes at Pearl)
> (Pearl waves her on)

So I want to tell you this now, so it won't make your
mouth drop open later.

> (Helen and Alice have a curious look on their
> faces)

I'm pregnant.

> (Helen and Alice are both shocked to hear
> this news)

Helen
Wait now. Her husband has been away in Alaska on the fishing boats for some time now.

> (Alice and Helen both get up from their seats and give Leola a big hug)

Leola
I just found out Friday that I am one month pregnant.

> (Alice looks at Leola)

Alice
Are you serious?

> (Taylor walks past Alice and stops on her
> Chair side)
> (Willie goes over to Taylor)
> (Willie is frustrated at Taylor but gives a fake
> smile)

Willie
Taylor, why I am doing your job?

> (Willis is headed to the kitchen to put dishes
> in the washing machine.)

Taylor
Maybe cause you good at it.

> (Willie continues to keep his cool)

Willie

Taylor, what is it man?

> (Willie extends his arm and shakes hands
> with Taylor)
> (Taylor is taken back by this gesture)

Are you alright? Are you working with me or not?

Taylor

Yeah, man, I'm cooler than a fan. It's these people.
There are too many things going on in here. I'm
alright though.

> (Taylor looks around to see the dinner
> customers then back at Willie)

Taylor   (con't)

Listen, man, I went out drinking and smoking last
night and I was higher than a kite.

> (Willie and Taylor walks to the wall where
> the kitchen door is)
> (Rene opens the kitchen door)
> (Rene walks between Willie and Taylor and
> looks directly at Taylor)

Rene

Willie, Taylor, you are so lazy.

Taylor

Here she comes again. You are always running your mouth.

(Taylor makes a hand gesture of a mouth talking)

Yeah, Yeah, Yeah, Yeah, Yeah . . .

(Rene points and shakes her finger at Taylor)

Rene

If you ever did any work around here, I wouldn't complain.

(Taylor rolls his eyes and makes a hand gesture that implies her to walk away)

Taylor

Just go back into your little cubbyhole, Rene.

(Rene has an insulted look)

Willie

Listen to me. Both of you! Taylor and Rene heads turn towards Willie. (He is speaking in a stern tone) You know how these people do me.

(Taylor and Rene are taken back by Willie's tone)

Taylor will you make sure to you help Rene keep these people quiet and orderly. You got to give them good service and maybe that will calm them down. (Willie hits his hand against the wall)

I need a drink!

> (Rene walks out of the kitchen to the main room)
> (Taylor puts his hands up towards)
> (Willie so he will calm down)

<u>Taylor</u>
Willie, I will help Rene. Tell me something though.
Why are you sweating these people so much man?

<u>Willie</u> (Yelling)
Will you just do what I said Taylor?

> (Lower yelling tone)

Just do what I said man.

> (Taylor is upset with Willie's tone but keeps
> his cool)

<u>Taylor</u>
> (He is Sarcastic)

Cool.

> (Taylor turns his cap backwards)

Talk to me that way, will you.

> (Taylor walks out of the kitchen door into the
> main room)
> (Taylor looks over and sees Rene. Rene has a
> bewildered look)

Taylor

Rene. Willie wants you to take care of that main table.

Rene

All right, Taylor, you know he told you to do it, you clown.

Taylor

   (He is frustrated)

Will you just do it, Rene?

   (Taylor and Rene are standing side by side)

Rene

You're going to get fired, Mr. Taylor.

Taylor

Oh, no I am not. You know why? Ask me why, Rene. Ask me why? (Rene has a look of irritation)

Rene

OK, why Taylor?

Taylor

It's because, I am much too smooth for that.

   (In a cool smooth tone)
   (Taylor bumps his hips with Rene's hips)
   (Taylor leans into Rene right ear)
   (Taylor is whispering)

Taylor (continues)

I'm too smooth.

> (Rene is extremely irritated but walks back
> to the cafe to avoid an argument)
> (Taylor gives out a big laugh)
> (Willie walks out of the kitchen door and
> walks over to Leola's table)

Willie

Let me go over and say hello to these women.

> (Willie stands in front of Leola's table and
> looks at all of the women)

Good afternoon ladies, good to have you here again.
Are you finding things to be satisfactory?

> (The women look Willie up and down)
> (Everyone is quiet for about five seconds)
> (Willie begins to feel nervous)

Well, let me know if you have any problems. Just let
the wait staffs know and we will take care of it.

> (Silence continues as Willie walks to the next
> table and waits on other customers)

Leola

Look at that man's feet! My goodness, let's sing the
feet too big song. Go-o-d ni-i-ight!

Alice

Leola, we just told you about your mouth. Come on now. You just left church and look how you're acting. You are going to mark that unborn child you're carrying. He's going to have a big watermelon shaped head and boat sized feet. (Leola makes a facial gesture of giggling).

>   (Alice glares at Leola who then makes a
>   straight face)

Leola

I can't help myself. It is so funny to me.

>   (Helen shakes her head)

Helen

She doesn't know what she is looking at . . . a man with big feet . . .

>   (Leola keeps giggling to herself)

Girl, where have you been? You ain't heard?

Helen

Anyway, I digress because she talks about men with big heads too. You would Think she's perfect, let her tell it.

Leola

Especially, if they have that big, gigantic question mark shaped head. That started with Michael McGee. You know that head stretched from the corner of 5th street, all the way to 6th Avenue and around the corner. I mean . . . and now that they shave their heads, I laugh all the time. People think I'm crazy, just call me happy, call me happy. Leola pauses and turns her towards Helen Oh; oh . . . here comes Willie again. He's got that nosey look on his face.

> (Willie walks over to the table with more confidence)
> (It is noticeable by his proper posture)

Willie
Hello, again ladies. Are things alright?

> (Willie smiles and looks directly at them)

Are there any problems? You're a little loud . . .

> (Willie pauses for a few seconds)
> (He clears his throat then continues)

I mean it's a little crowded in here? If you need anything, call me.

> (Willie looks at Helen since she is close to him)

Helen
No, Willie, everything is fine.

> (Willie stares at Alice who begins to feel uncomfortable)
> (Alice gives Willie a forced smile)

Alice
Everything is fine.

> (Alice looks at Leola and Helen who both look at her)

Big foot!

> (Leola and Helen let out a laugh. Alice makes a smirk)
> (Willie is unaware of what the women are talking about)

Willie
Well, if you need anything at all.

> (Helen, Leola, and Helen calm down their laughter)
> (Willie walks towards Rene)

How is everything going Rene? Are you OK?

> (Willie is about to put his hand on Rene but hesitates)
> (Rene notices but doesn't make an issue of it)

Rene
I'm OK. Just not in the mood for any of those women today. (Rene shrugs her shoulders), but I'm good. I still have to get food orders from their table.

<u>Willie</u>
Just be professional and if that doesn't work, just pray.
But, hold your tongue. We need the business. They
may be loud, crass, obnoxious and tired; but they pay.

Do you know what I'm saying?

<u>Rene</u>
I know. I'll do what I have to do.

<u>Willie</u>
Thank you, now, where is Taylor?

>   (Willie turns his head around)

Let me go find this boy.

>   (Willie rubs his forehead with his hand)

I need a drink today.

<u>Rene</u>
Drinking!? What does that have to do with . . . ?

>   (Willie cuts into Rene's talk)

<u>Willie</u>
Never mind that, Rene. Just tend to those people and
hurry them out of here, will you? I wish I didn't have
to deal with this every Sunday.

>   (Willie pulls an order ticket out of his apron
>   and looks at it)

Lord, have mercy.

> (Willie puts the ticket on the ordering table)
> (He sees Taylor coming out of the employee
> bathroom door)

<u>Willie</u>
Taylor, where have you been? I have been looking all
over for you, Taylor.

<u>Taylor</u>
> (He is so sarcastic)

I was in the rest room, if you must know. I told you
that I went out drinking last night. I think I might
have caught a little too much something.

> (Willie has a disgusted look on his face)

<u>Willie</u>
What, boy, I don't want to hear about that. I thought
you meant something else.

<u>Taylor</u>
> (Taylor is using a Joking tone, but he is being
> a wise guy)

That's what you get for assuming. I went drinking,
like I said. I didn't say anything 'bout anything else.
Let me go to work. By the way, I heard you going on
about needing to go out drinking.

> (Taylor gives out a big smile)

Really man, you should go. What are you doing
letting these people in here every week, if they bother
you so much?

Willie They pay.

> (Willie's face has a look of despair)

And we need the business. Why are you talking up for
them all of a sudden?

Taylor
Well, they are just people. Everyday people, church
going people, with problems just like the rest of us.

You have problems too, don't you?

Pastor Wright
My God, my god, they don't have a clue. When they
find out, what will they do? They're faking. It will
only break their hearts. Too many faces playing too
many parts. One day they will find out just how it
feels to be dropped, deceived and rolled down a hill.
I hope they have Jesus on this dark and messy day, if
not they deserve it, tips fall where they may.

> (Rene is standing at Leola's table) (She is
> holding a coffee container and is pouring
> coffee into the cups)

Rene
Okay, here we go now, coffee all around, condiments
are on the table.

Leola

Yeah girl, my husband . . . is a hard-working man. But I loved the attention he stopped paying to me too.

> (Leola puts cream and sugar in her coffee, while she continues to talk)

He knows I am a woman who needs lots and lots of attention. I needed all that attention he was giving to those dang sports.

> (Helen and Alice both put cream and sugar in their cup, while listening to Leola rant)

He is replacing me with some sports and work. No, no, I am not having that. I am a Christian woman but I need my husband's attention.

> (Leola puts her hand through her hair)

Night and day, day and night, you feel me girls? I need it!

> (Rene runs over to the table and interrupts the ladies conversation)
> (The women are taken off guard)

Rene

Ladies, let me know if you need anything else, I'll be right over there at my table counting receipts.

Leola

The nerve of some people, it is hard to find good help these days.

Alice

Humph, she just ran over here and just broke into our conversation

Helen

Calm down girls. You know where you are.

> (Helen looked around, so she wanted to see if people around them could hear their conversation)

Leola

Anyway, yeah, girl, he knew. Leola doesn't say anything for a few seconds. And what's that song that was out years ago.

> (Leola gets up from her chair and moves around the table)

Talking about,

> (Singing)

The same thing it took . . . to get your baby hooked . . .

> (Helen and Alice join her)

Helen and Alice

It's going to take the same thing to keep her.

> (Leola sits back down in chair in an upbeat mood)

Leola

You know it!

Helen

Sounds like tough times came kicking in your door.

Alice

I hate it when that happens.

Leola

Girl please, being ignored even when I was really in the mood. That Tough time was working overtime. I tried to resist, because I love my husband. But tough times just didn't want to leave my home. My husband got it too good to have me starving for it, so I thought about it and you know temptations started to scream with that loud voice. I wanted any kind of attention by then. So I went to tough times for comfort. I didn't even know many of the brother's names, temptation, that's the baby's daddy.

> (While Leola keeps talking, Pastor Wright is walking by Leola's table)
> (Alice and Helen continued to drink their coffee because, they wanted Leola to continue with her conversation)

I went back to my husband because old tough left me, when I got pregnant.

> (Pastor Wright stops and looks directly at Leola)

Pastor Wright What?!!!

> (Leola eyes become wide since caught off
> guard)
> (Leola looks back at Pastor Wright.)

Leola
Sorry Pastor, my husband thinks it's his child. I don't function well, without my husband. Leola puts her hand on her stomach.

Leola
He knows my needs very well. It freed me to go to him, all that stuff is gone now. I was able to confess it.

> (Serious tone)

Yes, all of it. Now, I have my husband back and he really is the best thing I ever had.

Leola
He is just a little . . . so . . . boring . . . excuse me, I have to go to the ladies room.

> (Helen pulls Leola back into her seat while
> Alice and Pastor Wright block her way)
> (Leola has an upset look on her face)

Helen
Oh, no you don't! Don't try running away now. You don't have to go to now ladies room. You are always the one with that, "I got an opinion about your business attitude". You always think that you know more than anybody else. You always want to direct

and control everybody. Now you are going to hear our opinion.

> (Leola sits back down after Helen pulls her back) (She uses a stern tone)

At least you're going to hear mine. Now, I have called you many things Leola, but co-dependent was never one of them. Are you alright, girl? I hope that you are truly free of those tough times sister.

> (Helen smiles and sits down)

Leola
What?! I just told you, I'm fine. I really am.

Alice
I think that we should just leave it alone. Let the ISMS die.

> (Helen looks at Alice with a disgusted look)

Helen
That's because you think you got it all under control too. But, you faking it just like the rest of us. I know what I am talking about. See you all don't know my story. Alice walks towards Helen.

> (Alice is clenching her hands and making fists)
> (Helen notices and begins to look defensive)

<u>Alice</u>

Oh, girl, we know how you like to be the center of the universe. Like your story is all that. Helen points her finger at Alice.

<u>Helen</u>

See, that's not even what I'm talking about.

(Alice points and waves her finger as well)

<u>Alice</u>

Then what are you saying because, inquiring minds want to know.

<u>Helen</u>

(Yelling)

Look! Ms. Thing, I didn't come in here with you today to go through this again with you. I have told you before.

(Pastor Wright stands between both women. (Taylor can be seen cleaning a table close to them)

<u>Pastor</u>

Sisters!!! We need to sit down and be civilized. This is a place of peace and I will not allow any sort of violence on any day. For that matter, today being the holiest.

(Taylor stops cleaning a table and walks over to help Pastor Wright)

(Taylor stands between Leola and Helen)
(Leola gets up from her chair and moves over to Alice)
(Taylor leans in to flirt with Helen)

Taylor
I just wanted you to know you look very pretty today.

(Alice and Leola roll their eyes at Taylor)
(Alice looks at Leola)

Alice
Let's see how smooth he is.

(Both begin to smirk and try to contain their laughter)

Taylor
(Taylor is getting nervous as he approaches Helen)

I know you probably heard Rene saying how lazy I am and all that; I'm not like that in everything.

(He is regaining his confident)

I'm really good.

(Taylor gives Helen a wink from his left eye)
(Alice and Leola wink three or four time at Taylor)
(Taylor gets embarrassed and gets on the defense)
(He makes a motion with his hand)

Oh, that's how it is . . . ?

> (Taylor puts his hand down and starts to relax)
> (Pastor Wright sees the atmosphere has changed and sits at an open table)

Oh, okay. I got some things to say. I know your story, Helen. As I said before, my father knew your father. I remember him too; they drank a lot and talked loud. So your father spilled a lot of beans on you Helen.

> (Helen scratches her forehead and looks at Taylor)

Helen
If you got something to say, then say it.

> (Taylor pulls a chair from the other table to Leola's table)
> (He sits on the chair and looks at Helen)

Taylor
I have always liked you. I thought that you were real nice, you know? Your father was so ashamed. He thought you were spoiled. He said things like, "yeah, she was born with a silver spoon in her mouth." Helen starts to get upset but tries not to show it.

> (He is being sarcastic again)

He said things like that. He said stuff about your friend.

> (Helen begins to have tears in her eyes)
> (Taylor sees this and changes his attitude)

(Taylor is being a jerk with a serious tone)

Your girlfriend, that, you were close to. Love is like that, you can be so close to someone, that no one can make you see the truth about that person you love because you love them and love is blinding.

> (Taylor pauses for a minute and hands Helen a napkin to wipe her tears)
> (Helen takes the napkin and puts it on the table)

Your father said you'd get angry every time he tried to pull you away from her. I get it.

> (Helen wipes the tears with her hands)
> (She takes a deep breath and looks directly at Taylor)

<u>Helen</u>
> (Helen is upset now)

You don't know my story. I'll tell it. I have repented and I am saved now, Taylor. I'm not afraid anymore. Truth sometimes will make you angry, it's deep inside, you know. I care so much about everyone. Every year, I would find a school and donate toys to every child at Christmas. Never took anything in return. I just like doing that. It kept me from wondering about when I was going to receive love, someone to really love me.

> (Helen pauses for a few seconds)

Have love for me. I made a mistake. One day I approached my friend, I confessed my feelings for her and we entered into a relationship. After a while things started to change, something was different. We were searching for something. It landed us in church. We found there was a power greater than any love we had known or imagined.

> (Helen turns looking and talking at Pastor Wright)

Helen

Now, that I was living in the truth, I told the Pastor about my desire to be with a woman. He prayed and we prayed.

> (Helen is on the kneeling on the floor where Pastor Wright is sitting)
> (Pastor Wright helps her up)
> (Helen gets on her knees again Helen is sobbing and talking)

I remember getting up off the floor of the church. We were praying and I just remember getting up off of the floor of the Church Later, we got baptized. Now I am a missionary spreading love all over the place. I still remember my friend Regina.

Taylor

Whatever happened to Regina?

Helen

She was killed by a man, years ago. A man, who was supposed to love her, I still weep, but instead of feeling the anger . . .

>(Helen clutches the cross necklace she is wearing)

I pray.

Taylor

Wow. I never heard this, Helen.

Helen

Not something I like to talk about.

Alice

We all have ISMS but each is different.

Jessie

Glory, Glory! Good afternoon everyone! How goes it?

I just got out of church and I feel like shouting "Glory"! Did you all go to Sunday morning service today?

>(Jessie waves hello to everyone in the cafe and walks through from)
>(Jessie continues to walk through the room)
>(He seats himself at the left table)
>(Jessie walks past Pearl)

Pearl

Hey . . . Jesse, let's talk. I got an open chair right here.

Jessie

(Yelling)

Ms. Pearl, I think that I am going over there and sit
with the "Billy goats"

> (Ms. Pearl laughs)
> (Jessie sees Leola's table and walks toward
> them and he stands in front of them)
> (Jessie points at each of the women at Leola's
> table)
> (Leola stares at Jessie) (Jessie stares at Leola)

Did see you all at Sunday morning service today?
Yes . . . No . . . hmmm

Leola

You know you saw us at Sunday morning service,
Jessie! Stop showing off, everybody sees you! Sit your
little scarce tale down.

> (She is irritated)
> (Jessie smacks his mouth with his hand while
> looking at Leola)

Jessie

Well . . . praise the Lord. I'll just go over there and sit
with the Pastor. He's got the spirit.

> (Jessie sees Pastor sitting at a table in the
> same room and alone)
> (Pastor sees Jessie and tries to avoid eye
> contact by looking into the menu)

(Jessie walks on over to Pastor Wright)
(He is very cheerful)

<u>Jessie</u>
Good afternoon Pastor.

(Jessie grabs a chair and sits in it)
(Pastor Wright puts the menu down)

<u>Pastor Wright</u>
I'm doing good Jessie . . . and yourself?

<u>Jessie</u>
I'm just great. I feel the power of the lord today.

<u>Pastor Wright</u>
I'm glad to hear that Jessie. I'm very glad to hear
that . . .

<u>Jessie</u>
There is something I wanted to ask you.

(Pastor Wright looks at Jessie)

You have excellent sermons. You really do. I just feel
their too rehearsed.

(Pastor Wright has an upset look on his face,
but he keeps his cool)

<u>Pastor Wright</u> Go on Jessie.

<u>Jessie</u>
I mean no disrespect but we know very little about you.

I am just speaking privately, one pastor to another.

Pastor

I understand your concern but I still need to adjust to this area. I confess I still have some growing to do in my calling.

Jessie

Still Pastor, I hear people gossip. How you speak from the book but not from your life.

Pastor

Perhaps you're right Jessie. Everybody has a desire to know, who their pastor is. It comes with time

Jessie

Look. Let me tell you about me.

(Jessie stands to get everyone's attention)

Listen y'all, let me tell all of you about me.

Leola

Well . . . I was waiting to hear who you are. I have been watching you. You look like you got some ISMS.

Jessie

I had a breakthrough a while back and my life never was the same. If I can get a breakthrough anybody can. Now I don't feel the need to revisit the old ISMS. God has transformed my thinking. I did it all; women, drugs, pimping . . . the gambit. I was good . . . I was real good at it. I enjoyed it. It was a big old game to me. It was one that paid very well. Humph . . . jail, that is where I found time to stop and see if this God thing was really what it was cracked up to be. Well, I shouldn't a done that because he showed up and showed out. It didn't take a long time either. So anyway, let's do what the Pastor says, we should do. I know we are going to be blessed by doing it. I believe that.

> (Jessie sat down and continued to talk to Pastor Wright)

<u>Pastor</u>
The Lord is doing an excellent job in bringing souls back to himself

<u>Jessie</u>
You sure are Pastor doing a good job for the Lord. I just felt we needed to talk. This is one pastor talking to another pastor. As someone spreading the word you know we are . . .

> (Jessie is interrupted)
> (A cell phone ring is heard)
> (Jessie reaches into his pants pocket and opens it)
> (Jessie turns away from Pastor. He answers the call)

Hello . . . I'll be there shortly . . . yes, about 15 minutes. All is well then, bye now

> (Jesse turns back to Pastor)

Well, I've got to go preach at another church, so I need to be getting on the road. I just stopped by.

Pastor
Before you leave . . . you were going to say something
else.

Jessie
Another time Pastor Wright

> (Jessie goes to the front door he completely
> ignores Pearl)

Pearl
Some people . . .

> (Pearl continues to sip her coffee)
> (As Jessie exits, another person enters the café)
> (It's Butch staggering, entering down stage right)
> (Leola sees Butch and shakes her head while
> her hand is on her forehead)
> (She is laughing out loud and then points at
> Butch)

Leola
Will you look at this? There is old drunken Butch.
Lord, have mercy.

> (She stares at Butch and looks at Alice)

Look at him . . .

> (Leola makes a four finger gesture for Butch
> to come over)

Come, come, come . . . come here Butch

(Butch sees Leola's hand)

Come here Butch. Butch, look at you! Have you been out drinking all night again? You have, haven't you?

(Butch stumbled over to Leola)
(Alice's facial expression is of disgust)
(Leola is chuckling)

Butch
Shut up Leola! I came in here to see Helen.

(Butch looks at Helen lovingly)

That's my Helen.

(Butch walked over to the main table and began to hover over to Helen)

I knew you'd be here, baby.

Helen
Leave me alone, Butch. Leola, why did you call him over here? You know how he is girl. Leola is now laughing while Alice is chuckling. I don't have time for you today, Butch. You will embarrass all of us. Go over there and sit down. Get yourself some coffee or something.

Butch
Coffee!? I don't drink coffee. I thought you knew that? I want some whiskey, girl. I served my country, I want a decent drink of wet whiskey. The only wet

things I want on these lips are whiskey and your lips, girl. Right now, I am half way to having both.

Helen

> (Upset)

Sit down somewhere Butch.

> (Butch staggers and sits at the table down stage left)
> (Butch talks as he is walking)

Butch

Girl . . . I'm the best thing in this place, you better ask somebody.

> (He turns and looks at Helen before he reaches his chair)
> (He sat in his chair and stares at Helen)
> (Butch stands up straight and touches his shirt's sleeves)

You know you want me, girl. Yeah, you do. You want me. I can see it in your eyes. A man knows these things

> (Butch rubs his head with his right hand)
> (He then licks his index finger to clean his eyebrows an. Butch then points to him)

You want *ME*, baby

> (Butch winks at Helen)

(Helen stares at Butch)

Helen
Just sit down Butch and stop winking at me before I put something in that eye . . . like my fist

(Everyone laughs out loud)

Butch
Not till you leave with me right now

(Helen ignored Butch and started talking about herself)

Helen
Here I am, trying to hold on. I'm over the dang hill, overweight, still over sexed . . . over qualified for most jobs I seek . . . and no man want me.

(Everybody points at Butch)

Everybody
Butch!!!

Leola
Butch!!!

(Butch looks away)
(Alice and Leola laughs)
(Helen begins to become irritated)

Helen

Ha, ha, ha, that's funny. The average man is
intimidated by me. I'm done. I'm over it . . . I'm over
it. This is not funny anymore.

> (Helen cries in her hands for 10 seconds).
> (Butch's face is sad and wants to touch her
> hand)
> (Helen's tears but sees his hands are dirty)
> (Butch puts his hands in his pockets)

Butch

Aw hell, Helen, you are too sensitive baby. You don't
weigh but a pound. If I blow on you too hard, you
would fly away like a peacock feather.

Helen

Why today of all days? Butch then looks directly at
Leola.

Butch

Leola, see what you started. I ought to snatch that wig
off your head

> (Butch reaches for Leola's wig)

You are messing with the wrong woman.

> (Leola moves with lighting speed. Leola gets
> up from her chair)

Leola

I wish you would B-B-B-Butch! That was close. I
almost called you something else.

Butch

If you do, I'll tell Pastor Wright on you. (Yelling) He's right there. I'll just turn around and I'll tell him.

> (Butch turns around and point at Pastor Wright)
> (Pastor Wright's back is turned against him since he is talking to Pearl)

Leola

> (Yelling)

Some military man you are. Can't do nothing by yourself.

> (Butch has reached his highest level of anger by now and calmly walks behind Leola and snatches her wig off while she is still talking)
> (Everybody laughs out loud (Leola grabs her head)
> (Leola's eyes pops wide open)
> (Leola's mouth flies open)
> (Helen and Alice try to help her put her wig back on)
> (Pastor Wright walks over and is in front of Butch)

Pastor

I just saw what you did, Butch

> (Pastor Wright looks directly at everyone in disappointment)

I've heard all of your commotion. It is hard to be out in public with you and you are my church members.

That is embarrassing . . . unfortunately.

Butch
See, I told you!

> (Butch turns his attention back to Helen)
> (Pastor Wright turns and walks over to stage left)
> (Pastor Wright puts his hands on Botch's shoulder)

Pastor
Go ahead and sit down Butch. I hope I don't have to conduct a sermon right hcr.

> (Butch sits down while Pastor Wright takes his hands off Botch's shoulders)
> (Helen stands up from her chair and looks at everyone at the table)
> (She then sets her eyes on Butch)

Helen
I look at you Butch and it reminds me of how blessed I am. I think about what God has done for me and how he set me free. My soul cries out, "Hallelujah".

> (Helen begins to sing)

Helen
I know I've been changed I know I've been changed
I know I've been changed I know I've been changed
I know I've been changed I know I've been changed
Angels in heaven done signed my name.

> (Alice takes the second verse of the song)

Well if you don't believe that I've been redeemed you know the angels in heaven done signed my name. Oh Follow me down to that old Jordan stream Angels in heaven done signed my name

Pastor
Oh I stepped in the water and the water was cold. It chilled my body, but not my soul The Angels in heaven done signed my name.

Helen
I know I've been changed, I know I've been changed,

Oh Glory, I know I've been changed, Angels in Heaven done signed my name Angels in Heaven done signed my name.

> (Helen stops singing. Butch pulls his chair close to her)

Butch
Helen, tell me the truth. Do you really believe in God?

Helen
Yes, Butch, I really do. If you knew my story, you would understand why.

Butch
Helen, listen to me for a minute. I'm serious now. If I find God, would you consider me?

Helen
No! If you are finding God for me, you are wasting your time. Find him for yourself.

<u>Butch</u> (shocked)
Find him for myself!!!!?

<u>Leola</u>
You need to do that, right now, that is the truth.

> (Leola clutches her cross necklace)

<u>Alice</u>
Amen!

<u>Butch</u>
Helen, you're wrong about yourself.

<u>Helen</u>
What did you say to me?

> (Butch leans in toward Helen from his seat)

<u>Butch</u>
Your ISMS, my Helen, is that you try to tell people what they see and don't see in you. You are insecure even with all that you have going for yourself. I will use five seat belts to keep you from falling out of my ride. I am a keeper, baby! Ask somebody!

<u>Helen</u>
You see there? That's the devil adding in his two cents. Lord please have mercy! You don't even have a ride butch, you crossed eyed donkey!

> (Butch sees everyone in the diner laughing at him)

Butch

Hold up Helen, this ain't no devil talking to you. I am a man in love with a woman that I want to marry.

Helen

Be quiet with that talk, Butch. I don't want you, man

>(Willie walks on over to see what the commotion is all about)
>(Helen sees him, stands up and directs a question at him)

And Willie, don't you laugh. I've heard about you, my brother. It is men like you who don't have respect for a woman's body. Look at your scars on your own face.

>(Willie puts his hands on his face and gently feels the scars)

It came from so many fights with women . . . didn't it Willie? You remind me of Regina's ex-old man.

>(Helen is looking around at everyone then Helen sits down)

Was I gay without a reason? Is this an ISM? I remember what she went through.

Chapter II Scene IV
The Statistic

FLASHBACK TO: REGINA

She begins to sing, "Jesus loves me"

>(SINGING)

Jesus loves me, this I know. For the Bible tells me so.

Little ones to him belong, we are weak, but he is strong. Yes Jesus loves me, yes Jesus loves me, yes Jesus loves me For the Bible tells me so. (Song ends)

<u>Regina</u>
Bobby will be here soon.

>(The front door is heard being open) (Bobby enters the room)
>(He sneaks up behind Regina and stands there for a minute)
>(He is wearing a skull cap and a red jacket)

<u>Regina</u>
I love my man.

>(Bobby sneaks closer behind her and hugs her waist)
>(Regina is startled. Her mouth drops and her eyes pop)

<u>Bobby</u>
Hey girl, what have you been doing today?

Regina

Just cooking and cleaning, the things you like, Bobby.
Bobby, I have been thinking . . . let's start going to
church. I was going before we met and now I don't
go at all. I have been feeling the need to get closer to
God.

> (Bobby grabs Regina close to him from the
> front)

Bobby

Gina, now you know that I am not a church boy. You
knew that when we met. What's up? Are you trying to
change me now? You don't like me the way that I am?

Regina

Well, sometimes you get so angry. You make me
nervous, Bobby. I don't know what to do when that
happens. I think God can help us with that. I love you
and I want us to work.

Bobby

Listen Regina . . . I am not messing with God and
I don't want him messing with me. We have a good
understanding

> (Bobby looks around and he let go of her and
> pushes her)
> (Bobby points his finger to the window)

Bobby

Is that right? Is that right? Just like the man across the
street, huh?

Regina

No, Bobby! Don't do this today, not today. I cooked your favorite. You are making me nervous, Babe.

Bobby

You a lie, you know you a lie. This house isn't even clean.

> (Bobby grabs Regina by the throat and moves his face close to her face)

Regina

I did cook, it's in the oven. Don't do this Bobby.

Regina cries.

Bobby

I make you nervous? I make you nervous? I'll show you nervous!

> (Bobby raises his hand to slap her)
> (Regina raises her arms to protect herself)
> (Bobby punches Regina in the stomach)
> (Regina falls to the floor)
> (Regina puts her hand on face)
> (Bobby turns his back away from her)
> (Regina begins to cry)
> (Bobby shakes his head in disgust).
> (He then turns his body back at her)
> (Bobby's hands are waving all over her head)

I know you been messing with that man across the street. I am not stupid.

Regina

No Bobby, You are wrong. I didn't.

> (Ruby's voice is heard coming in the house
> while Bobby slaps Regina)

Ruby

Regina . . . ! I brought you this dress, babe!

> (Ruby comes in, walking on her cane)
> (Regina falls to the floor. Ruby enters the room)
> (Ruby runs to Regina and holds her)
> (Ruby drops the dress she is holding in
> hangers in her right hand when she sees
> Bobby beating Regina)
> (He is hitting and kicking her)

Ruby

> (Yelling)

Bobby! You leave her alone. I will kill you, Bobby.

> (Ruby clutches her cane and points it at Bobby)

Do you want to fight a woman, Mr. Bobby Davis?
Okay you fight me, fight me, boy.

> (Ruby stands looking down on Regina and
> looking straight at him)

She has never done anything but be nice to your
rotten tail. Fight me, boy. I will kill you.

> (Ruby keeps a firm grip on her cane)

Bobby
> (Yelling)

Go on now, Ruby Lee. She needed a beaten so I gave her one.

> (Bobby points his finger towards the window)

Messing with that man over there, I know it. She got a smart mouth too and I am not putting up with that.

I'm out of here. I can't take it no more

> (Bobby walks from one side of the living room to the other side)
> (He exits)
> (Ruby follows him to the door)
> (Bobby stops walking and raises his fist to Ruby)

Ruby
> (Yelling)

So help me, Bobby, I wish you would touch me, I would . . . Lord will you help me!

> (Bobby stares at Ruby to intimidate her)
> (Bobby shakes his head and slams the door)
> (Regina's grunting on the floor)
> (Ruby locks the front door and runs back to Regina)
> (Ruby grabs and holds the telephone, binding down at Regina's side to console Regina in her arms)

Ruby

That darn boy, this is the third time you're going to the hospital because he keeps losing control. I know what's going on. I'm no fool either! I'm calling the police.

> (Regina touches her bloody lips with her hand and then feels her bruised stomach and grunt)

Regina

No, momma, don't call the police. He didn't mean it! He didn't know he was hurting me. I lied to him. He thought I understood his instructions. This is my entire fault.

Ruby

Even if that was the truth, and it isn't, a grown woman can't take that kind of pain day in and day out, let alone a young girl. Sadistic is what it is, another statistic.

> (Ruby uses the clothes she is wearing to dry the tears from Regina's eyes).

Ruby

Just relax Regina. I won't have it, he must be stopped.

When I should have stopped him, I didn't.

> (Voice cracking)
> (Ruby starts to cry and the tears come down her face) (Ruby sings the song "His eye is on the Sparrow")

I sing because I'm happy, I sing because I'm free, for His eye is on the sparrow and I know He watches me.

FLASHBACK ENDS

> (Pastor moves to Helen and consoles her by patting on her back and looks up)
> (He then looks at everyone at the table with his head down)

Chapter III Scene V
No ISMS

Pastor
I can tell we need to pray. We need to pray to god. See God already knows and he is just waiting for us to bring it all to him. Father you are going to have to help me with these ladies and these brothers.

Alice
Willie, what is your truth? Tell Helen what really happened? Don't you lie either, cause I'll bust you in your eye. I will too! I was told about you. My story is similar to what happened, just like with Regina.

Willie
Helen that was over twenty years ago. I sympathize with you, but I'm not that Bobby dude.

Helen
It didn't make sense, Willie. She finally had to go to the hospital for surgery and never came out alive, so yeah, I have an ISM about that, my brother. If you

can't be gentle, then just you and your bad intentions
stay away! I'm scared to death of men in my bed,
Willie. She loved that boy and now she's dead.

> (Pastor Wright hears his cell phone ring in
> his pants pocket)

He pulls the phone out and reads the text.

Pastor
Pardon me everyone I need to take this.

> (Pastor Wright walks out of the room)
> (Willie pulls a chair from the other table) (He
> pulls it towards him and close to Helen)
> (Willie looks at Helen)
> (Willie puts his hand to his hand on his chest)

Willie
I didn't even know him or Regina for that matter. So,
don't hold me responsible. I'm trying to keep my head
straight. Leola cuts into Willie's conversation.

Leola
Wait a minute! Back the train up. Did I hear that
right? I knew it. I knew it! All this time, all your big
talk about all this sex, but you never once showed up
with a man, Helen.

> (Leola makes a hand gesture of stopping)
> (Helen has a look of frustration.)

Well, I'll be jumping up and down for you. I respect
the truth, really, you my girl Helen. I got you.

<u>Alice</u>
She doesn't respect nobody and she is going to somebody.

<u>Helen</u>
She's going to tell anybody.

<u>Pearl</u>
She is going to tell everybody.

>	(Leola waves Pearl off)

<u>Helen</u>
Is that right, Leola? Like the good book says the truth is the what?

>	(Helen looks at Leola to finish her sentence)
>	(Leola is taken back an unable to answer)
>	(Helen continues with her dialogue)

I'm alright now, I celebrate the truth, Alice. How about you?

>	(Alice nods yes)
>	(Butch walks away)

<u>Butch</u>
>	(Yelling)

Oh my goodness. I feel dizzy.

>	(Butch starts acting and clowning)
>	(Butch grabs his heart on the right side)

Leola

That is not the side where your heart is, Butch!

(Butch looks at his heart and his eyes get big)
(He quickly changes hands)

Butch

I'm coming, daddy! My blood pressure is going up!
My woman . . . My Helen . . . is gay? Helen, don't you
feel sorry for me honey? Don't you feel like hugging
me some?

I'm the best thing in here. Come on home with me,
Baby. Take care of your man

(Helen waves him off)

Leola

Calm down, Butch! You really drank too much last
night.

(Leola stares at Alice)

Now Alice, I know that you have something that you
have been hiding from us. What's your story? Tell us.

What is in your past?

(Alice is looking around the cafe to avoid eye
contact with Leola)

Alice

I'm a Christian now, Leola. I don't want a bad
reputation. I'll leave it like that.

Leola
>   (Condescending tone)

Oh! You're a Christian.

>   (Angry tone)

Well, what does that make us, Alice? We attend the same Church service as you do, so don't even go there. If you live the truth, speak the truth. Pastor just . . .

>   (Alice cuts off Leola's conversation)

Alice
Ok, Ok . . . I'm free of it anyway. It's all past trash, old ISMS, so yeah.

>   (Alice shows strength as she stands and
>   walks around the restaurant)
>   (She walks back to her seat)

Crack cocaine, Heroin, alcohol . . . for over 10 years, is that what you want to hear, Ms. Leola?

I sold my body to support my habit.

>   (Now Alice has tears in her eyes and looks at
>   Leola with anger)

You know Leola, it is mighty strange that you are always digging around, looking for something negative to say to bring some other person down. Why do you always have to feel better than everybody else? I am I a better place right now, because God delivered me. Let me finish my story! You want to know.

> (Leola and Helen remain quiet while Alice vents)
> (Alice grabs a napkin from Rene and wipes the tears from her eyes)

That was before I received my grandmother's estate. That kept me up to the chase, I mean, I could afford my habit. I found out real soon that I had inherited more than my grandmother's estate. I inherited a lifelong companion named H.I.V.

> (Helen and Leola have a shocked look on their faces)

I was later delivered from the disease, purely by the grace of God.

> (Taylor overhears the conversation while walking around taking orders) (Taylor walks over to Pastor Wright)

<u>Taylor</u>

Let me ask you a question, Pastor Wright. Is there a cure for H.I.V.?

<u>Pastor</u>

There is no cure, yet. How old are you, boy? I want you to go get educated on these diseases in this world. People are dying every day because they don't know what is what. Abide by the laws of the Bible. That is the safest way to stay away from these types of disease.

Taylor

No! I just thought about Alice. Pastor she experienced a miracle. She could have been dead. That's all I know

Pastor

Listen everybody, Taylor just asked me if there is a cure for HIV. I want you all to hear. This is a disease that is most times sexually transmitted or transmitted by unclean injection needles. The scientist and doctors are working on finding more vaccines for this disease. It's a horrible thing to have happen to anyone. Please keep that in mind.

> (Pastor Wright walks over toward Leola's table)
> (Alice gets up from her chair and stops Pastor Wright at his tracks)

Alice

Pastor . . . I had . . . I was HIV positive

> (Alice looks away and then back at Pastor Wright)

Pastor

Lord, have mercy. Alice, do you need . . . ?

> (Alice cuts him before he can finish)

Alice

Yes, Pastor, you do . . .

(Alice's face is showing sadness)

It's been years now, I have the Lord, but, I do need someone to talk to.

(Pastor Wright gives Alice a hug) (Taylor watches the conversation with his hand on his jaw)
(Rene also watches the conversation from the counter with her right hand on her hip)

Pastor
Amen . . . we are more than conquerors through him, my daughter. Amen, he loves you Sister Alice and we are praying for you, all of us. Amen . . . Amen

(Pastor Wright nods to everyone at the Leola's table)

Willie
Alice, I don't know what to say, I am sorry.

Alice
Don't be sad for me, I am delivered now. I'm living. God is a blessing. I was scared of dying so, I hired professionals to take care of my needs. If I hadn't hired a smart broker, I would be broke today with those kinds of medical bills. Praise God! God blessed me. My mother was on crack cocaine. She came home high and bitter quite often.

Taylor
Ms. Alice, is that for real? That is so hard to imagine. You are so petite and innocent looking.

Leola

Don't worry, Alice. You are alright. Many other people are in the same boat that you were in. Some of them might be right here in this room. You would never know, you can't tell by looking.

> (Leola looks at Pearl)
> (Pearl reacts by pointing at Leola)

You are healed, right? I mean . . . you are healed, right?

Alice

Yes, I am healed now. She and my step father fought all the time. Knives, bats and guns, it didn't matter. One day my mother shot that stupid man right in the butt. I laughed so hard and so long, that, I thought I would lose my breath. He was most angry that I say it happen to him, than he was that I saw a bullet lodged in his big round ashy butt. I was glad cause that meant that he couldn't touch me like he did for a while. I told my mother about his attacks on me and instead of her offering a decent way out, she offered me a temporary fix, her crack pipe! My own mother got me hooked on crack cocaine. I was only 14 years old

> (Alice stares at Leola)
> (Butch walks over to Alice)

Butch

Alice, don't make that face. You look like a pug, you ever seen a pug? They're the cutest little dogs. Look like this.

(Butch is pressing his nose to the side)

Alice
Butch! I am not Helen.

Helen What?

(Alice catches herself and looks at Helen then Butch)

Alice
I'm sorry Helen. Butch, I'll come over and tie those big jumbo ears in a knot so tight that you will be able to see around the world.

Butch
Um hmmm . . . you are getting too old to do those acrobats with that rubber neck.

Leola
Leola, give me my purse, so I can beat this man up. He must be crazy to be talking to me like that.

(Alice moves in on Butch)
(Willie and Pastor Wright keep them apart)

Pastor
Alright now saints, stop acting like heathens. Let's maintain a level of dignity and respect, after all, we are in a public place and we are of Christian belief. We aren't a bunch of wild animals. You are working my nerves, now!

(Everyone looks at Pastor Wright and music
starts to be heard)
(Everybody except the Pastor, sing a song about
how everyone is pushing them to be crazy)
(Everyone except Pastor starts dancing and
singing)

All   **(Singing)**
Don't push me 'cause I'm close to the edge. I'm trying
not to lose my head, Pastor Wright jumps in.

Butch
Uh huh-huh-huh

All   **(Singing)**
It's just pathetic sometimes, it makes me wonder
sometimes . . . How I keep from going crazy

Butch
Uh-huh-huh-huh-huh

All
It's pathetic sometimes, it makes me wonder
sometimes . . . How I keep from going crazy.

     (Pastor walked back to his table while people
     stare at him)
Pastor
Now sit down!

     (Everyone sit down quickly)
     (Willie catches Pastor Wright before he gets
     back to his seat)

Willie

Pastor, will you pray for me? After hearing all these ISMS, I need to clean my plate formally. I'm Willie. I did some bad things in my life. I didn't always go by the name Willie. I hurt some good people.

Pastor

Go on. I'm listening.

Willie

I hurt my own daughter and wife. It's hard for me to even say it, but I know I need to come clean so I can heal inside. I got my ex-wife hooked on drugs really bad. Can God forgive me for that, can he Pastor?

Pastor

Yes, he can and yes, he will. Just ask him in earnest, he will forgive you.

Willie

I feel the need to tell you folks my story. I need forgiving too. I was raised in a ghetto in California, I fought almost every day because I didn't want to join a gang. Surviving meant fighting harder and harder. Soon I became hard. I watched people depend on drugs to help them forget the stink and the poverty and the loneliness around them. It got to me too, so I used . . . I took advantage of those who were weaker. My dad was a big time drug dealer, so I learned firsthand how to be the best. I was good. I was the best on the block dealing my wares.

> (Willie is now standing between Leola and Helen)

(Willie then looks directly at Alice).

Alice, I've been watching you. I've been trying to make sure that you were alright.

Listen . . . I was young Alice. I was just trying to survive. I didn't know how it would affect you or anybody else and I really didn't care, as long as I got the money. I shouldn't have done that to you, to anybody. Then, I was an addict and it really didn't matter anymore. Can you understand Alice? Will you try to forgive me? Try, Alice. When you're in that place, all you can see is the fastest way out of it and so we were all lied to about the drug. Before I knew it, I and your mother were strung out . . . stealing, writing bad checks, abusing and misusing people who cared about us. Things got so bad, I didn't know which way was up and before I knew what I was doing, I was abusing my own little girl.

> (Alice stares at Willie) (She slowly starts to recognize him)
> (She slowly stands up, moving toward him with wide eyes)

Alice
> (Shock with her mouth and eyes wide open)

Oh, my Lord . . . !

Willie
There were many days when I was coming off a high. I wanted to just kill myself for what I was doing.

(Willie beats his chest and begins to cry)
(His voice is cracking)

I was so messed up, Alice. I loved you; I was just so messed up.

(Willie wipes the tears from his eyes)

Your mother tried the best way she could to love you and me. I was just so messed up.

Alice

(Yelling)

Lord, have mercy . . . Oh, my God.

(Alice tries to runs out of the cafe with the speed of a runner)
(Willie hits a table but continues to goes after her)
(Willie chases after Alice and grabs her arm)
(She pushes him away)
(They are still in the restaurant)

Hey I have got to get out of this restaurant. You are not my father.

Willie
Yes, I am your father.

Alice

(Yelling)

You are not my father, Willie!! You didn't have any part of my conception!! You abused me!!

Willie

I am your father, Alice. I am the only father you know. Our family had good times too.

> (Pastor Wright grabs Willie by the shoulders and tries to have him let Alice go without causing a scene to attract attention)

Alice

> (Yelling)

Youuuuuuuu! Oh, my God!!! My life has been a living hell because of what you did. Oh, my God.

> (Alice points her finger at Willie)

Pastor, you get this man out of my face or start praying right now.

> (Alice slaps Willie in the face)
> (Willie takes the hit and does not fight back)

Alice

Mama killed herself, you know that? She couldn't take it anymore and she just killed herself off, leaving me to fend for myself. You want me to for forgive you? You forgive yourself, let God do the forgiving. I hate you for what you did our lives.

> (Willie begins to cry)

Alice

Was it worth it Willie, Was it worth it? Oh, my God, help me! I have to get out of here, this is too big of a test for me right now Father God. I have to get out of here.

> (Alice uses all her strength and pushes Willie)
> (Alice runs into the lobby singing "I must tell Jesus")

Song:

I must tell Jesus all of my trials;

I cannot bear these burdens alone;

In my distress He kindly will help me; He ever loves and cares for His own. I must tell Jesus! I must tell Jesus!

I cannot bear my burdens alone;

I must tell Jesus! I must tell Jesus! Jesus can help me, Jesus alone.

> (Alice stands in the middle of the lobby looking around)

Pastor Wright

You all stay here. I will go and talk to Alice. Lord, have mercy on us this day.

> (Pastor Wright runs into the lobby and Alice turns and hugs him)

<u>Pastor Wright</u>
Alice . . . Alice

<u>Alice</u>
Please help me

<u>Pastor Wright</u>
Alice. Listen to me.

(Alice falls on her knees and starts to pray)

<u>Alice</u>
Our father, which art in heaven, hallow would be thy name, thy kingdom come, let thy will be done on earth as it is in heaven. Give me this day my daily bread. Forgive me of my trespasses as I forgive those who trespass against me. Lord, deliver me from evil, for thine is the kingdom and the power and the glory, forever and ever. Amen

(Pastor kneels down with her)
(He touches her on the shoulder)

<u>Pastor</u>
Listen to me child. I know you think that this may be the worst thing to happen to you. God has a plan for you, Alice. This is not just something random

(Alice stops praying and looks at Pastor Wright)

<u>Alice</u>
Pastor, I thought God had given me a clear conscious regarding my past. I guess I still have sin in my spirit. I don't know if I can forgive him Pastor.

> (Alice begins to cry and her voice is cracking)

I don't know if I can deal. I thought God was . . .

> (Pastor Wright interrupts her conversation)

Pastor
Alice . . . when God forgives us, it is a done deal . . . There is no such thing as unforgiving grace. His divine duty, when we ask, is his complete forgiveness. It is up to each of us to find the power in ourselves to do the same. That is the test, my child. We all have our level of decision making in this walk of faith. Don't let the enemy still your joy, not now. Don't be robbed again after having come so far by faith. It is grace that seeks to free you right now child. You stand up and face the power god has given you to succeed.

Alice
Pastor . . . I don't have the strength . . . I don't . . .

Pastor
> (He is speaking in a firm tone)

You believe in the power of God. Do you believe in the power of God?

Alice
You know that I do, Pastor.

Pastor
Then let's go inside, have a bite to eat and perhaps a cool drink. Let's let his power feed you the truth. We

are more than conquerors in him and I know where
I've come from. Amen.

Alice

Alright Pastor, I do believe in the power of god. I have
overcome so many things. I know with my faith in the
almighty and you standing with me, I can do my best.
Since, God has given his best. Alice wipes the tears
from her eyes with her hands.

> (Alice is having difficulty getting up) (Pastor
> Wright sees this and helps her up to her feet)

Alright . . . alright

Pastor

That's the spirit, Alice.

> (Alice and Pastor Wright walk into the cafe
> and back to Alice's seat)
> (Alice sits down quietly still wiping tears)
> (The other customers are looking at them and
> sees Pastor Wright waves his hand at Rcne)
> (Rene walks over to him)

Pastor

Rene, please bring Sister Alice a ginger ale and get
some food on these tables, please.

Rene

Are you okay Alice?

Pastor

Could you please get the order while I talk to my people here?

>(Rene has a surprised look but follows Pastor Wrights order)

Has everyone ordered? Let's eat, I'm hungry now. Praise the Lord.

>(Alice looks at Pastor Wright with a puzzled look on her face)

Alice

Pastor, you said something out there a few moments ago and it has me wondering.

Pastor

What was that, Alice?

Alice

Remember, you said from when's you came. Pastor, from where did you come? What was your life about?

>(Pastor avoids the subject by looking deeply at his menu)

Pastor

Let me look at the menu, I am hungry Saints. What are you all going to order?

>(Helen and Leola quickly picked up their menus and chatter about the food)

Willie

Alice, forgive me if I bother you too much but, can I have just a few minutes with you alone? I really have something to say to you.

> (Alice puts her menu down)
> (She looks at Willie and sees the sincerity in his eyes)

Alice

Alright . . . Willie, alright!

Pastor

Do you need me to follow you out there, Alice?

Alice

I'll be alright.

Pastor

Are you sure? Willie maybe you can talk to Alice in front of us?

Alice

Thank you Pastor. But I'll be alright.

Pastor

Alice, uh . . . because of the circumstances, I insist that you remain in this area

> (Alice looks at Willie who is nervous)

Alice

O.k., Pastor, I think you are right. Talk here, Willie

<u>Willie</u>
I should have been there for you,

<u>Alice</u>
Alice stands up in anger.

<u>Alice</u>

(Alice starts to cry)

Why? Why Willie? So you could give me the hit yourself. So you could make it easy to have me all to yourself? She thought that she was saving me from you! You made her so pitiful and disgusted for you . . . She crawled around on all fours looking for drugs she thought you had for her. She was depleted because you abused and rejected her.

(Alice is so angry) (Willie begins to cry)

Even through the abuse, Willie, she loved you. You treated her like a dog. You made her pathetic. As sad and pathetic as she was, she loved me enough to throw herself at you like a lost dog to pull your focus away from me. Do you see why it's supposed to be hard? How can it be easy when you have so many scars to heal? I am going to do my very best to forgive myself and to forgive you, Willie. It is the only way to hold on to the love smiling at me in the Lord.

<u>Willie</u>
I am working to change everything about me now, Alice and I believe God has a place for my forgiveness too . . . I believe he does.

(Willie wipes the tears from his eyes)

This is hard for me to do because I don't deserve your . . . Alice . . . I really am very sorry for all I have put you and your family through . . . I know I have an appointment with God to face all I have done.

(Willie pulls out a picture of himself, Alice, and her mom from his shirt)
(He hands it to Alice)

Look at us, Alice. We had good times too. I really want to try and make it better in any way that I can right now, while I can look you straight in your eyes and say this to you. I was so messed up Alice. I loved . . . l love you still.

(Alice remains speechless and she looks at the picture, then she back away from Willie)

<u>Alice</u>
That's the first time that I've heard those words from someone in my past. Pastor helped me to see. I have an obligation to the Lord to forgive. It's not supposed to be easy or we would not need faith. I know it is going to take some time for you to completely heal from the damage that you have done, but this is the first step and I do forgive you, Willie. I forgive you for all that you have brought upon your life and the lives of others. Wait . . . I take that back. I forgive you for what you have done to me.

(Alice slowly walks back into café)

> (Willie stays outside silent and unable to move)

May God have mercy on us all

> (Willie and Alice are back in the café, from stage right)

Willie

Alice . . . thanks for the talk . . .

> (Alice looks back at Willie)

I want you to know this place here . . . this restaurant here is for you, too. I did this so I could one day give it to you. I really did . . . Well, will you excuse me? I have some work to finish in the back office.

> (Willie walks to the back office and Alice walks back to her Table)
> (Rene walks over to her table)

Rene

Ms. Alice, here is your ginger sis . . . now, what can I get you all to eat?

> (Alice looks at door to the back office)
> (When she picks up the menu to order she puts it back down)

Alice

I can't eat right now . . . please take the order for the others.

Rene
You should eat something. How about the house special?

Alice
Okay. Thank you, Rene.

> (Rene walks back to the kitchen)
> (Pearl walks over to Alice to console her by placing her arm on Alice's shoulder)

Pearl
Alice, I'm so sorry. I am praying for you. God bless you, dear.

Alice
I'm alright. I was just thinking . . . my mother. I was just thinking about my mother. I think about her every day. I really miss my mother. I remember screaming at my stepfather . . .

Chapter IV
Scene VI
No one saw my wet tears

Flash back to Alice as a child

> (Young Alice is sitting on the floor doing her home work in the living room)
> (Willie enters in a sly, creepy and quiet way)
> (Mary is not in the room)

Willie

Come here Alice, You know what I am here for. Come here and get this daily medicine.

> (Alice backs away from Willie)
> (Now Willie yelling to intimidate Alice)

COME HERE, GIRL!!! Why you always fighting me?!! You know you want this.

Young Alice (Yelling) Leave me alone. Leave me alone! You too big to attack a little girl! You do this every day, daddy! Stop touching me!

> (Willie begins to pull and push on Alice's arm)
> (Alice runs around the furniture)
> (Willie catches her and gets forceful and pushes Alice down)
> (They both tussle and Willie slaps Alice)

Stop! You're hurting me . . . daddy. Stop! No . . . I don't like this! You're hurting me.

Alice   (as an adult)

I was only 10 years old.

Young Alice

Momma! Momma! Where is my momma? No-o-o-o . . . stop . . . your hurting me!

> (Willie is now dragging Young Alice on the floor)

Alice   (as an adult)
I was calling my mother, but she could not hear me . . .

> (Young Alice is screaming loud enough for
> her mother to hear in the next room)

Young Alice
Why won't you make him stop? You are supposed to
protect me, mom. Make him stop!

> (Mary comes into the living room staggering
> because she is high on drugs)

Mary   (Yelling)
Where are my . . . ?

> (Mary sees what is going on)
> (Yelling)

Dang it!

> (Mary sees Willie trying to sexually abusing
> Alice)
> (Angry and emotionally hurt for Alice and
> herself)

Alice   (Speaking as an Adult)
I was scared every time my mother left the room.
We never went to church back then. I enjoy going to
church now . . .

Mary
Willie, leave her alone . . . what are you doing? Get
away from Alice!!!

(Willie rushes out of the room)
(Only Alice and Mary are in the room)

Young Alice

Momma, you got to' get sober so you can help us get away from here. I am scared every time you leave the room. He is evil momma. Maybe if you took us to church sometimes, things would be different.

Mary

I was hurt the same way you are being hurt, when I was your age. My mother didn't know how to protect me. Look at me child. I can't even help myself. Your dad and his controlling ways got me hooked on this mess. It controls me, he controls me and now he controls you too. Its life child, don't worry. Just push it out of your mind. The best thing to do is just forget about it. Here . . . let mamma fix it up for you, baby girl.

Momma is going to fix it up real nice for my baby girl. I'll take care of it baby. Momma will take care of it.

(Alice moves to the phone)
(Alice tried to pick up the phone to call Jessie, her friend)
(Mary follows Alice to the house phone)

Mary

Baby girl, who are you calling?

(Screaming loudly and nervously)
(Mary throws the phone down)

No, Alice, don't do it like that. Let me help you baby.
Momma's the only one who can help you. Here I fixed
it up real nice for you . . .

> (Young Alice is terrified and is walking away
> from Mary.)
> (She has never been afraid of her mother
> before this day)
> (Willie enters and Young Alice runs to her
> closet door)

Willie

What are you still doing here, woman? Look at you.
You look so pathetic.

> (Mary crawls up to Willie, and attempts to
> stand up)
> (She struggles, but she gets on her feet)

Mary

Come on Willie. Let's go to our room. I got something
for you . . . Let's get out of here.

> (Mary is throwing herself on Willie, hugging
> him close around his waist)
> (She is desperately trying to take his
> attention off young Alice)

Willie, look baby, look at me. I fixed myself up real
nice for you . . . I got something good for you. Come
on, let me show you. I got it good for you, Willie.
Come on now.

(She is dancing very provocative similar to a stripper)
(Willie is avoiding her advances and pushing her back, but staring at the closet)

Come on Willie!!! I know you like baby girl, but I got it for you Willie. Ain't I still good to you?

(Willie stands there and just stares at Mary)
(She sings "I can't make you love me")
(Willie and Mary continue to look at each other for a about 10 seconds)
(Willies slap Mary and she falls to the floor)
(Young Alice is in her closet, leaning against the wall)
(She is holding a blanket in her arms and looking down at the floor)
(She bursts out of the closet and runs to kneel down by Mary)

<u>Young Alice</u>
I love you momma.

<u>Alice</u> (as an adult)
Mom's offer came more frequently towards me. I finally tried it . . . After that, I was hooked and I bonded with my mom. I was a mess just like my mom . . . The burden of drugs and abuse took a toll on me. I slit my wrist a couple times. I lived, but in great misery.

(Mary rolls up young Alice's sleeve while They are sitting on the floor)
(Alice falls over and passes out)
(Mary began to cry as she struggled to get up)

Mary

I am so sorry, Alice . . . I can't do this to you anymore. I am so sorry. It's over . . . I can't live like this anymore. God, please take care of my baby

END FLASHBACK

Leola

I love you, sister. No matter what.

Alice

Thank you, Leola.

> (After Leola consoles Alice, Helen gives Alice a hug)

Helen

Sister, you have been through so much.

Alice

Thank you, Helen.

> (Pearl walks over to Alice and gives her a hug)

Pearl

Sister, you will never be alone. You got all of us.

> (Alice is quiet for a few minutes)
> (Alice takes a sip of the ginger ale)

Alice

There is a plan working here. I know it is!

(Helen and Leola put their hands on Alice's hand)

Pastor Wright Praise God.

Leola
Well, I understand that Pastor and I don't mean any harm, but there is still the issue of . . . let me say it this way, men have a tendency of . . . well, wait a minute, I mean.

(Taylor is irritated that Leola won't say what she means)
(Taylor interrupts Leola's speech)

Taylor

(Sounds very irritated)

Leola, say it, just say it . . . say it.

Leola
I believe if we were able to listen to one another in a real way without all of the "men" for a lack of better words . . . Issues, things would change. You know what I mean?

(Leola sees Butch staggering around the café)
(Leola turns to Butch and just stares at him)
(Butch gets up and walks over to Leola)

Butch

Don't look at me, Leola

> (Butch points his finger at her)

Leola, it is folks like you, who make men like
me who we are. I am constantly trying to escape
foolishness, but, it is everywhere I go. Can't people
choose one real thing to fulfill their lives and just
cling to that thing? Why is it necessary to talk
down to others or talk about people that you don't
even know, let alone understanding their what they
are going through . . . Humph . . . you all need
Jesus more than I do. At least, I may be a drunk,
but I really do know that God is real. I just need to
accept what he wants me to do. When I give my
commitment to him, you better believe . . . . It will be
on like popcorn, baby.

God's word would be just popping out of my mouth

> (Butch makes popping sounds 3 times)
> (He looking like he's in deep thought)
> (Butch chuckles)

All I do is stay drunk. I don't talk bad about nobody

Leola

That is the jive that I am talking about. That's why
you don't have a woman. You drink too much. No
woman is going to put up with that very long, Butch!

> (Pastor Wright gets upset and defends Butch)

Pastor

Leola, that's enough, now

Leola

Do you see? That is part of the issue now. Whatever it is, be it drinking, control, mental, sexual or physical abuse . . . Whether it is sports . . . whatever, money or whatever keeps us divided in the listening and really hearing one another.

(Butch looks irritated but continues to stare)

See all women want from her man is the know we are on his mind and to have his attention, at least, some of the time but more than just a little every now and then.

Butch

You shut up, Leola. You do not have my story right. I am very loving but.

(Butch pauses for a few seconds)

Helen won't marry me and Leola. You run your mouth so much, that everybody have to struggle to get a word in, edge wise . . . I will snatch that wig off of your head again, Leola. You get on my nerve so-o-o bad.

(Butch attempts to snatch the wig but falls on his floor)
(Everyone at Leola's table laughs at Butch)
(Willie remains silent and helps Butch up)

Alice
Come on you all. This is ridiculous.

Pastor Wright Butch!

(Butch let them help him up)

Butch
In case you all want to know . . . I have dignity. I am a drunk, with dignity. I'm a former marine. I don't need any help. I speak from the heart . . .

(Butch goes to the cafe's rest room)
(Alice and Pastor Wright look frustrated)
(Pastor sits back down in his seats)
(Jessie returns to the café)

Leola
Now Pastor, I heard Alice's question that was directed to you earlier. What did you mean by "From where have you come?"

Pastor
Listen, Leola . . . I don't have to tell anyone what I have done, except God. Now I believe that we all have been through enough here today.

Leola
0-o-ow, Pastor Wright, do you mean that we don't know who our Pastor is?

(Helen joins Leola and Pastor Wright's conversation)

Helen
We want to know you too, Pastor. Talk to us now. Have you ever done anything wrong in your life that you regretted and had to repent for? You should tell us.

Pastor
Alright, Leola, Alice, I receive that. Now the question becomes, are we using our own wisdom?

Are we living the example? You see, I am a faithful man and I live the example now. I am now doing something different than I used to do. When I was married, I loved my wife so much.

Let me tell you, she was one of a kind. She always kept my attention. She was a bad Mamma Jamma.

ALL
Mamma Jam ma?!

Butch
Mamma Jam ma!

> (Butch said it in a smooth and hip way)
> (Everyone is happy now)

Pastor Wright

> (Pastor Wright's mood changed to sadness)

Yeah! She was so inviting. She always had her hair, finger nails and toe nails done. Her hair was never the same. I always had the same woman, but a different woman. I never got tired. She would dress in different ways. One day she would took sophisticated, one day she would look sensual, one day she would dress boyish, and I was never bored. I had a hard month and it was back on December of 1990. It was about Christmas time and I had lost my regular job. I wasn't a preacher yet and Christmas was around the corner. We had four little beautiful girls. They were all daddies' girls. I just didn't know how I was going to make a Christmas for them. I looked for odd jobs, but no one would give me a job. She was so patient about everything and she went to work to keep the bills paid. I was frustrated one day and she was late coming home. I got so insecure, for some reason. I accused her of another man.

(Jessie butts in on Pastor's story)

Jessie
Um hum . . . she knew you were lying, didn't she?

Pastor Wright
Yes and I knew that I was lying. She defended herself and proved that I was lying. My goodness . . . I, uh, I, Lord help me. I hit her. Now, I already knew that if I ever hit her, I would lose her. Her daddy taught his daughters that if a man ever hit them one time, he would do it again. Even with that, she mentally left me and it never got right again. She tried to please me, but I became more demanding and she had a nervous breakdown. She left and never came back.

Leola
Is that all, Pastor Wright?

Pastor Wright

No, Leola. When she left me, I was on my own. I had
to survive, so I started selling drugs. I got caught and
served time in jail. That is alright . . . because, that is
where I found God. I came out preaching with a new
story. Amen.

Leola

The Lord sure works in mysterious ways. My big old
mouth might actually pay off today. Hallelujah

> (Alice is standing alone in the restaurant)
> (Alice looks all and sees a book on the floor
> and she picks up the book)
> (Alice began to read it)

Alice

The evil one saw the God in our hearts, we were like
lambs while doing our parts. Unlike the evil one who
twisted the truth, he said I know Jesus, but who are
you? They looked with tears, the fear they dread, no
words spoken, they can't go to bed Jesus suffered
persecution, his life was at end, but they are blessed
because he rose up again. He is our brother and he is
our friend, who needed words when he rose up again.

Leola

Pastor, why do you think ISMS are associated with
loneliness?

> (Pastor Wright stares directly at Leola)

Pastor Wright

The older we get the lonelier we become. Perhaps we should listen more, give positive healthy criticism maybe, taking responsibility for our actions, seeking a true understanding of faith principles, discretion, forgiveness of us and each other. It's all a part of the recipe. Love is the ultimate result. So, to answer your question, Sister Leola . . . I don't know.

> (Pastor Wright then looks at everyone at the table)

What I do know is when we are going through and we see another day, we have to thank God every morning and that is great news. Well, I am going back to the church house. You are welcome to come back, if you like.

> (Pastor Wright gets up from his chair)
> (Butch gets up from his chair as well)

Butch

May I be able to say something, please?

Pastor Wright Go on Butch.

Butch

You changed, huh? I am a guy, just like you, but I need a lot of work still. I want to go to church with you.

> (Everyone to stare and be silent)

I am serious. I am a good man. Maybe Helen and God can clean me up.

Leola
Go on now, Butch. You get on my nerves.

Butch
Well, you all get on my nerves. You won't let me sit with you. I have to scream for everything.

> (Butch starts to walk toward the door and turn his head to see Helen).

And Helen won't marry me. That is wrong, plain wrong. You watch, next week I am going to be sober and I will be in church with my Helen.

> (Butch points at Helen)

I'm working on you, baby.

Jessie
I think I want to be there if only to see that.

Pastor
Come on Butch, I am taking you home. Let's go buddy.

Butch
Helen.

> (Butch blows Helen a kiss)
> (Pastor Wright and Butch walk towards the front door and exit)

Butch

Pastor, I need a favor . . . uh ruh . . . can we go by the store?

Pastor Wright

No, Butch, we can't. I am going to pray for you, Butch

Butch

Please pray for me, Pastor Wright. You see that I need it.

> (Willie sees Rene and Taylor and makes
> a hand gestures for them to come to him)
> (Rene and Taylor walks towards him)

Willie

Rene and Taylor, you two close the restaurant early.

> (Rene and Taylor look at each other)
> (Both then look at Willie and high fived)

I mean right now.

Taylor

Yes! Co-o-l.

Rene

Hey ah, ah do we still get paid for our regular hours?

Willie

You will Renee.

> (Willie gives Taylor a stern look)

Pearl

Lord you never cease to amaze me. Thank you for this most glorious day. I'm enjoying it so much I wish I could go to church with the Pastor for a refill. I must get home to my husband. Praise the Lord anyhow . . . everything is going to be alright. Renee, I want you to order something real nice for Leola next Sunday.

Rene

OK Ms. Pearl. What is it?

Pearl

I want you to order a specialty called SHOD UP!

Renee

I don't think we carry that here Ms. Pearl. Can you spell it for me? I'll try to find it.

Pearl

Don't worry about it baby. I'll bring my own . . . but, just for the record you spell it S.H.U.T.U.P. I'm going to throw a side order of it right down Leola's throat if she comes in here with that entire ruckus next week. Bye baby. See you at church next Sunday . . .

Rene

Honestly, I hated to see you all back here again, but I am glad now, I have even seen myself today. Is this really how it is? God accepted you after all that you've done . . . I can see a great change coming for me . . . I want that kind of change too . . . I want to go back to some of the people I know and share this kind of change. We all can use more of it.

Alice
You will get it baby . . . God has already heard your cry . . . you just made the first step, Renee . . . you know there is more of it next door . . . come on in and get his guidance. You two girls go on now, I'll be on later.

Leola
Are you sure Alice?

> (Leola looks strangely at her, then Willie and back at Alice)

Alice
Well, alright, you are a big girl.

> (Leola reaches for Helen's hand and pulls her toward the door)

Leola
Come on girl, I want to talk to you about this baby

> (Everyone except Alice Renee, Taylor, exits)
> (Willie returns to the restaurant)
> (Taylor rushes by Willie to exit the restaurant)
> (Willie stops in his tracks and looks at Alice)
> (Alice looks at Willie)

Willie
Alice . . .

Alice
No, Willie, don't say anything.

(Alice sings about how her change is going to come)
(Everyone joins Alice in singing)

So . . . the story ends but. If I were you, I'd want to know more about the environment of each of these characters. In other words, I'd want to know what makes them "tick". They all grew up in the same neighborhood, went to the same schools, attended the same church, but, they all had dark secrets that nobody knew about. Tell me, who knew? Why didn't they know? Just like many families, they didn't want to air their dirty laundry.

Chapter V—<u>Details on the characters</u>

About Alice

A nickel bag was bought here and a dime bag was bought there. That was child's play. I came from a line of drug users that didn't have a chance to give up. It started with my own mother and my step father, who I couldn't fully forgive and I am still praying for forgiveness for my hatred of them. My lack of forgiveness causes me to get physically sick sometimes. I get migraines so bad at times and I stay wake nights at a time for no reason. I find myself toiling to forgiveness and I stress because I can't forgive them. The lack of forgiveness that I am speaking of is dangerous to my health and safety.

My mother was hooked on heroin and my father was her supplier. Oh . . . I am feeling tears coming as

I tell this story. I have cried for so long now. It has been over 20 years. What is wrong with me? This is my flesh and blood! Just tell me how you would feel if someone you thought love you knew you were being raped every day and they didn't try to help you? Right!!! Betrayed!

I was only 10 years old with no help and no way and a fractured understanding of God. I'll tell you how it felt to me. It felt like someone was taking a meat clever and slowly ripped away the inside of my body from inside out. It felt like a tornado landed on my heart and began flinging the debris of my love for my parents to the outer limits. Couldn't my parents care more for me, even if they were on drugs? I hate drugs!!!

The last time he raped me, I told my mother about I didn't like it. She was so high on heroin that day and she looked like a bag lady from the street. She didn't bath or brush her teeth and when she answered me I felt **like throwing up.** Her breath was so bad. She said that I should notice how she looked and that she was like that because her mother didn't care for her properly. She said that, what she was going through was a part of life. I didn't want this to be a part of my life. I had nightmares all the time and one kept coming back to me . . . I dreamed of slitting my wrist in my closet, but I couldn't die. I always woke up disappointed because I woke up.

She offered me drugs all the time. I wanted to run, but I just couldn't leave her like that, especially with him. I didn't know what he was capable of doing to her. One day, I was so depressed and my mother offered me heroin. She told me that it would make me forget all of the bad things, so I let her give me the heroin. She gave me so much that I passed out. When I woke up I was so scared that I called my friend Jessie. Jessie came but, my step father, Willie, would not let him in. I found out that Willie got mad at Jessie and had one of his girlfriends to report Jessie's mother (a prostitute) for child neglect and he became a ward of the state. I went to my mother to tell her but she told me she couldn't do anything about it. She said that Willie owned her and she made it worse by saying that Willie owned me too. This time, I asked her for heroin, hoping that I would die. When I got high this time, I called 911. The police came, the ambulance came and the community was in an uproar. I went to the hospital and guess who was there when I woke up? My friend Jessie was there with tears in his eyes. He held back the tears because he thought that a man should never cry.

Jessie
Alice . . .

   (He spoke softly)

I thought that I was going to lose you. I thank God for keeping you alive. I know that I am only 12 years old, but I love you, Alice. You are like my sister. You know I never had brothers or sisters. I am glad you are alive.

Alice

Why Jessie? Why am I still alive? Now, I have to go through all of the same things that I was running from. I wanted to die. My step father is raping me, Jessie. My mother gives me heroin. I feel weird right now, because I want heroin again. Jessie, I am very confused and nervous. My body is cramping. What does this mean? Oh, God, please help me. Help me and Jessie to get out of these people's lives.

Jessie

You took too much of that heroin, Alice. The first time you called me. I did come, but your father answered the door and said that you couldn't have visitors. I could hear you singing so I left. This time you defended yourself, Alice by calling the police. Your mother and your father are under arrest. They tested positive that you were being raped and you will have to go to court to testify against them. You will do it, won't you, Alice? Don't save them, save yourself.

Alice

I am not going back, Jessie. You don't know half of the story of my nightmare. Everything was bad there in that house. Not just drugs and rape, but guns too, Jessie. My mother got mad at Willie one time because he wouldn't get her a fix of heroin. She found his gun and shot him right in his big, old, round and ashy butt. (Alice and Jessie started laughing out loud) If I go to a foster home, there is no guarantee that I won't go through this with total strangers, Jessie. Why didn't my parents just keep it simple and go to church, pray and live decent lives. Why didn't they show me the right path? Right now, Jessie, I am guessing about

God. I mean . . . I know that he is real. I don't know how to reach him. Jessie, Jessie . . . we need him right now.

Jessie
Look, girl, you are so strong. You do know how to reach God. Didn't he save your life? Yes! Do you have to go back to the same home of danger? No! Am I here with you right now? Definitely! What did you pray for Alice?

Alice

That God would get me out of that house

Jessie
Well, did he? Yes! You must have gotten God's attention.

Alice
I guess so Jessie. Thank you for coming to see me. I am very tired. I am scared to go to sleep though. Will you stay until I fall to sleep?

Jessie
Well, my old situation wouldn't have stopped me, but these new parents are caring for me, Alice and I don't want to get shuffled around to another home. I'll stay a little longer, but I have to leave soon.

Alice
Thank you Jessie

(Alice fell asleep quickly and Jessie left)

Alice became a ward of the state but she kept up with
Jessie and they ended up living in the same town.
Alice found out that Jessie had been sent to a home
where the father was a drug dealer and a womanizer.
It landed him in jail and landed him in East St. Louis,
Illinois.

Now, Alice told Jessie that he didn't know the half
of what was going on in her parent's home, but she
did not tell him about the night she had planned
to kill Willie. Alice was intelligent beyond her age
and she never liked Willie from the beginning. She
never told anyone that she had planned to wait until
her mother went to sleep (Mary, her mother was a
deep sleeper) before she executed her plan. Alice
knew a teen age boy in the neighborhood, who was
known for robbing homes and she plotted with him.
He was going to knock down the door and she was
going to hide in the closet next the door, waiting
for Willie to come outside the door looking down
the street and shoot him on the porch. The boy
would take Willie's watch and wallet, and then run.
Willie's name wasn't on the house lease or utilities.
Everything belonged to her mother and her mother
paid everything with her welfare check. They would
think Willie was a stranger, breaking into the home.

Well, there was an issue that came up. The boy had
gone to church the Sunday before this was supposed
to happened and repented for all of his wrongs. God
certainly had a hand in this. He saved three people at
once. I keep saying that God is multi-dimensional.

Her friend told her about his experience with going
to church and invited Alice to attend the service with
him. She made up every excuse in the book until he
became forceful. He was tired of her excuses so, one
Sunday morning he just showed up at her home early
enough to give her time to get dressed for church.
He even brought breakfast with him to eliminate
another possible excuse for not coming to church with
him. Alice got so nervous about the ideas of going
to church and simply said no. He explained that her
fear was a spirit on the inside of her that needed to be
confronted by prayers. He continued to tell her that if
this were not true, then she would not be afraid. Alice
became determined to confront this fear and went
to church with him. She was so happy when she got
home she went to the Christian book store and bought
herself a Bible. She read and she read until she fell
asleep. One night she fell to sleep after reading and
she had a vision. She dreamed that she was standing
in front of a crowd of people and everyone had on
royal blue clothing, with gold tassels on their sleeves.
From the crowd came a man whose clothing instantly
changed to white. He had on white shoes and there
was white hair in his temples. She listened in the
dream for sounds and the only sound she could hear
was moving water, like that on the beaches in high
tides. When the man opened his mouth to speak, a
flood of water poured out and went into her mouth.
She felt as though something filled her stomach. She
looked down at her stomach and her abdomen was
clear and she could see through her stomach. She
looked up at the man and tried to speak, but the only
thing that came out of her mouth was water. It seemed

as though words were being placed in her mind and she began sweating. She could barely contain her excitement. The next Sunday she went to the same church. The Pastor told Alice things about herself that she had told no one. She already faced the truth about herself. Now, she is finding herself confessing her wrongs to a man that she didn't know, but felt so close to. He also told her one thing that got her attention. He said, "The Lord told me to tell you something". She said what is it, Pastor?" He said, "From out of your belly shall flow rivers of living waters". Alice began shouting and crying, just thinking the fact that God is going to use her. The next thing she remembers was getting up from the floor and people around her was fanning her to cool her down.

You see, the dream that Alice had was a dream of deliverance and purpose. The water going into her mouth in the dream was the pouring out of God's spiritual anointing into her soul. You must understand that she was receiving the will of God's spirit into her very soul and she accepted the calling on her life to become an Evangelist. Being able to see the water in her abdomen was a sign that she would receive the gift of discernment. At this point she realized that she had been forgiven for all of her sins and that her faith was sealed. She rejoiced that she would no longer use alcohol, drugs or tobacco. She was delivered and healed of a disease that could have killed her. Some people would find it hard to believe that this was God's doing. I challenge the non-believers to open your mind and challenge God to magnify himself to you in your life. If you look for the good things, instead of looking for the bad things, you will see him in action. If you are too busy to keep on praying while you wait, you are doing it wrong. Don't stop your job, but take a few minutes in each day to say thanks to him, even before you receive your blessing.

Pastor as a Preacher

I have a poem that I want to open with, so that you might understand who I am.

Lying in the pulpit
I'm a believer in the almighty God
I find it difficult of just a bit hard
To understand people, when they ask why
"They" preach on holiness and turn around and lie

Lie, meaning fabricating and even one resting
Most of all, it consists of one missing a blessing
Don't you get caught up with church folks playing
Be for real, know the deal and hear what God is saying

I lied when I was throwing a fit, taking a hit, trying to get . . .

But, I would never lie like they do; behind the pulpit
God is worth it, don't lie in the pulpit. Be a lion in the pulpit!

When many people speak about Jesus, one of two things cross their minds; the torture that he bared or the betrayal that lead to the torture. The most popular questions are: Who is he any way and who is his real father? First, I would like you to realize one thing; God is truly his father and Jesus is God's *ONLY* begotten son. Jesus carried a very heavy message that many were not able to bear or receive. Jesus carried a message of deliverance and salvation.

Moses was a man of God, who listened to God's instructions and he fulfilled the mission or calling (of the purpose) on his life. All of those, who are purposed y God had specific jobs to do. Jesus was more than a prophet (in my belief) Jesus was the main part of a master plan, even before his birth. He was purposed to do work that no prophet or man could do. He had to deliver the world from sin. Yes, I believe that he was born of a virgin. I believe that he died and rose again on the third day. Listen to this; there have been people who were declared dead by doctors, but they can back to life. Some of them declared that they saw a very bright light at the end of a tunnel, but would not walk into the light and they came back to life. Do you believe this can happen? Well, why couldn't this have happened to Jesus? Neither story is more bizarre than the other. Do you agree? There are so many more amazing events that happen around the world that the average person never hears about.

I heard a while back that scientist have written news reports that states the earth is getting dimmer and that Chicago is sinking. Do you believe that? I'm making a point here and that is; people believe what they choose to believe. One thing I really desire for you to believe is there are greater events coming that will surely devastate you. The Bible says, "In the last days, the sun will refuse to shine". If you want more guidance, read the Holy Bible in the New Testament of Matthew, the 24th Chapter. It will amaze you. It speaks on the future of the earth. You may choose to believe it or you may choose not to believe it. Sure, some of the things have happened before, but the Bible did not say that it would not happen over and over again. One thing for sure is that the occurrences are more intense than ever.

I just wanted to turn to the side for one moment to point that out. Now, back to my topic at hand; Betrayal is spoken of in the Bible too. Throughout the Bible, you can find stories of betrayal. The Bible speaks also on sons betraying their fathers and fathers betraying their sons. The Bible says that in the last days, that is what will happen.

That makes me think about an incident that happened to me. I have been betrayed in my past and let me tell you, it was a hard lesson. I know that I am not innocent either because; I have betrayed someone that was very near and dear to my heart. It wasn't my father, it was my wife.

Pastor as a man

Confession is one of the most important roles of changing your life. After we've done what Leola did, that is; face the truth about ourselves, we may move on to verbal confession to God. It is a process of freeing your mind from guilt of the wrongs that you have definitely done. Let me give you an example. We wouldn't cook soup in a pot and reuse the same pot without washing it out first. What we would have a second dish of food that tastes similar to the first dish. I would say that the second dish was not purely correct. Can you see what I am saying here? It is very important to start with a clean vessel to produce a pure dish of food.

After confession, you may find that you need courage and strength against the temptation to return to your errors. Just keep praying. You are free but, you will have to fight to remain free.

I am a Pastor but I am also a man. I ask that you reserve your judgment of me, but you really don't have to because, I am free.

My life was not a life of good will. I have always been selfish self-centered. I will even say that I was arrogant. I had everything, education, good looks, a great body, a big fine car, a beautiful wife . . . humph (he paused) I just wasn't compassionate. I had four beautiful little girls, who I loved dearly. I thought that my money was speaking for me and I didn't have to show my wife the attention that she so desperately needed or deserved. I loved my wife but, I did not respect her. I was a broken man in a $500 suit. I did so much investing back then and money kept rolling in. One summer, I made a bad investment. I invested everything I had in this stock that was supposed to be fool proof. I was going to pull out of all of my investments after I collected the money. I remember it like it was only yesterday. It was like dooms day . . . The market crashed and instantly, I was broke. I didn't realize it then but, I had made a God out of the stock market. I watched it all the time, I waited for it to bless me with money, I prayed for success of getting the winnings. I guess God didn't like that. Today, I remember the scripture from the Holy Bible in the Book of Deuteronomy 5:17. T says "Thou shall have no other God before me".

I didn't do well after that. I began to avoid my friends, ignore my daughters and swear at my wife. One day, I totally lost it. It was in December and Christmas was coming up in a few weeks. I had gotten a little job, but it didn't pay for all of the bills we had coming in; the car not, the house note, insurance on the home and the car, utilities and food too. My wife had a job and she paid most of the bills. I felt so low and I lost respect for myself. She tried so hard to keep me content. I mean she did everything. She ran my bath water, cooked my meals, cleaned the home and took care of my daughter too. She worked long hours because we needed long money. I became stupid and insecure. I imagined that she was seeing another man and I kept on accusing her. I started fooling around on her and she found out. That night was so ugly. She was yelling and crying so loud and so terrible that I hit her, right in front of our girls. She grabbed the girls and I never saw her again. I heard that she had a nervous breakdown, but she had taken our girls to her mother's home. They refused to let me see them anymore and I was rejected by them on the telephone for years after they left. I don't know where they are today.

The moral of my story is; I needed God in my life and my family needed me to have God in me for guidance and protection for us all. Now, I have made a vow to God to stay on the path of righteousness and I will trust God with my life. Now that I have made this vow, I must keep it because he won't allow me to change my mind. He doesn't play.

Jessie
Don't send me away!

I was a man who had many fine girls
Working the street throughout the world
I was cool and sweet; sweet as honey
As long as the girls had my money

I laid them down when I got ready
One after the other, they came steady
I joked, they laughed—I could be funny, 'til one
forgot to give me my money

I rose up like a jaguar on the prowl
No one on earth could stop me now
I grabbed her hair and threw her down, the butt of my
gun hit her crown

I twisted her arm . . . oh, wow—it broke
The others got scared because I was no joke
They called for help and I gave them hell
They got me back by putting me in jail

In jail, I found that I needed a friend
Someone, upon whom, I could depend
Well, I didn't quite know how to pray
Somebody came to show me the way
First, I confessed that I had sinned
When I accepted him to be my friend
Next, I went to the chapel to pray

The Holy Ghost came to show me the way

I was baptized in a pool of cool water
My body got hot, I worshipped the father
I don't think I will ever forget
The day I said yes and my body got wet

My story is one that is clear. I was a pimp and I didn't
care about women. I didn't even care about my mother.
You see when I was a boy, I watched my mother leave
me as soon as dinner was over and I didn't see her again
until the next morning. I raised myself mostly, because
she would go to sleep shortly after she came home. She
used to smell funny all the time. I never knew what that
smell was. When she spoke, she always sounded like she
had been to the dentist and her tongue was swollen. She
couldn't walk straight half of the time. One day, I was
so hungry that I went to the kitchen to fix me a peanut
butter sandwich. I was about five years old. My mother
didn't have good silverware; about two spoons, one fork
and on butcher knife. That day I struggled to get the
peanut butter jar open. When I did, I started with my
finger to taste them individually. When I was finished
fixing the sandwich, I tried to cut the sandwich in half.

When I cut myself, I yelled . . .

"O-w-w-w, o-w-w-w, momma! I cut myself!" I
went running to her room. My blood was running
everywhere. A man came out of her room when I was
going into her room. I couldn't get her to wake up! I
couldn't get her to . . . wake up! I ran to the neighbor's
apartment, crying and bleeding. She stopped the
bleeding but, my hand throbbed.

It turned out that my father and this woman had fixed it so that the State Circuit Courts would take me from my home.

As the story continues, the police lady came to my house. The police lady said:

"Who is the head of this house?"

Neighbor lady
She is in there

Police lady
Will you tell her to come out?

Neighbor lady
She can't came out

Police lady Why not?

Neighbor lady
I need to take this boy to the hospital, you go in there

I saw her wink at the police but, I didn't know what that meant. The neighbor lady was taking me to the hospital and we talked.

Neighbor lady
What's your name, boy?

Jessie
My name is Jessie Walker and I am 5 years old. I'm going to be a businessman when I grow up, just like my friend's daddy.

Neighbor lady
My, you are smart, Jessie

Jessie
Yeah, you have to be smart to be a businessman

Neighbor lady
Do you have any brothers or sisters, Jessie?

Jessie
No, my momma said that I was a hand full by myself

(He laughed)

Neighbor Lady
What happened to your momma, Jessie?

Jessie
Nothing, she was sleep. Didn't you see her friend in our home? She was probably tired from his visit. She had just got home early this morning. She works at night.

Neighbor lady
Jessie, what if your momma went to heaven today?

What would you do?

Jessie
Nothing, I would just take care of myself until I get to be a businessman

Neighbor Lady
Wouldn't you miss her, Jessie?

Jessie

Nope, she is never home anyway. I never see her
except only a few minutes every day.

Well, I was in denial for years after becoming a man.

I had convinced myself that I didn't miss my mother.
I was convinced that I was just extremely mad at
her and we weren't speaking to each other. I was so
heartbroken and I missed her so much, but I had to
protect myself. I couldn't cry because I was a man
and I thought men didn't cry. In my secret room,
though . . . I cried, oh how I cried. You see I was still
a little boy who was left in a big world of strangers
and I was scared.

I found out some years later that my mother was
a prostitute and the man that I saw coming out of
her room was her pimp. My mother was murdered
because she didn't give him her money that night. She
had been saying all week that she didn't know how
she was going to get me some shoes and clothes. I
was about to start kinder garden and all of my clothes
were rags and I had no shoes. It was a mess, we had
no food most of the time. I might have eaten once a
day, my father left us because he was spineless and
had a black heart . . . calling himself a "rough neck".
He was a punk!

I was mad at my mother, still. I was mad at her for
not being a proper mother, for not having a father for
me, for not waking up when I cut myself so badly. In
fact I grew a hatred for women! I hated the neighbor
lady for calling the police lady who asked me all those

questions that a kid shouldn't have answered. I was
mad at that lady Judge who made me a ward of the
state! I was let down by *WOMEN.* They had to pay
for that. When I became a man, I vowed that every
woman, who came in contact with this tall, dark and
handsome chunk of a man; would pay dearly for what
every woman had ever done to me. I had them all on
drugs. You see, I was a big time drug dealer too. I
learned it from my father. Many nights and days, I hid
behind trash cans and bushes watching his drug deals
go down. I saw him beat up so many women but, I
saw men beat him up.

I told my ladies in the very beginning that I had trust
issues, but, they were stupid . . . every one of them.
When a man tells a woman that, she should run like
the wind. A man like that will kill a woman in the
name of love. They thought if they were sweeter than
any other woman, I would fall in love with them and
they would have me. Not a chance in hell . . . and that
is what I gave all of them . . . hell! I didn't know that
my lifestyle would nearly end my world. Sure enough
they conspired when they got tired of me beating
them down and they got me arrested. Most would
have thought that was my end, but, it was really my
beginning. I learned who God was and how much I
needed him in my life . . . right in prison.

Life was rough and I found out that that there was
always someone tougher than me. I had to find help
but I knew that it had to be from a source higher than
these guys. One day a clergyman came by my jail
cell and talked to me about Jesus. I didn't know who
Jesus was. My mother did not tell me about Jesus. He

kept on coming by, and then I went to the chapel with him for Sunday meetings. Who knew that I would be turned out by the word of God in the Holy Bible? I got baptized and now look at me . . . a new man.

Pearl

I played the piano for many years at the church. I sang sometimes and then I became the choir director. There were three women in church who knew they were not saved. I was tired of them parading around acting all holy. You could find them in the club every Saturday night. I have seen them walking to the club many times. They get in church and act like they are so pure. I got news for them; they don't fool Ms. Pearl. I got the Holy Ghost and he tells me all things. One thing for sure, I will do my best to keep them in line.

Pearl was the only child in her family as a youth. She was spoiled and very controlling. She was so happy to e a church member and that was for several reasons. One, she had other people to talk to, two, she thought could boss them around since she was the oldest member in the church and three; it gave her something to look forward to doing every Sunday and Wednesday. Pearl had a mission to safe other people, so when she sat in the pews, she would make sure she sat next to any visiting person who came to church or someone who looked like they were having problems. Pearl believed that families shouldn't have problems. She thought that every disagreement should be ironed out quickly. Pearl pulled many people out of trouble when she had a lot of money. The worse thing happened to her one summer.

Pearl had a cousin, who was convicted at an early age and sent to jail for armed robbery. Everyone thought that he was so sweat and innocent because he had good manners and he dressed very well. He always showed Pearl great respect and always hugged her. He was her heart. Pearl's heart was broken and the young man lost respect from everyone else in the family. Pearl believed that family should always be there for each other, no matter what the case was. So, Pearl spent several thousands of dollars on his books and many thousands on attorney fees. She did get him out of jail. Her grandmother had left Pearl all of this money, but it was dwindling away fast. She would look at her cousin sometimes and wonder what he would do now that he had a criminal record. She asked him one day. He had the nerve to tell her the truth. He told her that he would start selling drugs.

She did not like his answer and she hit the ceiling. She told him that; as long as he lived in her house he would not bring drugs or women in her house. He did not answer her because he had already started selling drugs and using them too. One day the phone rang and it was the police telling her that her cousin had been arrested for possession. Pearl cried so hard and thought about leaving him in jail, but, she went on to the jail and paid his bond and got him out. Pearl stayed calm on the way home, but when Pearl got this young man, who stood 6 feet tall and weighed 185 pounds, in the house, she attacked him like a football player and ended up having to call the ambulance to help him. When he got out of the hospital, he straightened up. He started going to church, got a

good wife and a good paying job. Isn't that what God
has to do to some of us? When he blesses us and we
take it for granted and ignore his instructions . . . he
will give us a good old fashioned beating specially
designed for us. Pearl gave her cousin some of what
he wanted and some of what he needed.

Ruby, Regina, Helen and Bobby

Ruby is my name. I am probably one of the more cold
hearted characters in the No ISMS restaurant. My life
has been hard and that hardened me to the degree that I
wouldn't allow myself to love anyone. I didn't take any
stuff from anybody, baby. I have beaten the heck out of
women and some men. Don't get me wrong though. I
never went out to start trouble, but if you bring to me,
I'll send it right back where it came from. No, I don't
regret anything that I have done. Well . . . maybe one
thing; my daughter. (She loses the tough attitude and
becomes remorseful) I didn't take care of her right. I
wasn't there for her as she was becoming a young lady.
I wasn't there for her to tell her not to let men touch her
in the wrong places, I wasn't there for her when she
started her menstrual cycle or grew breast. Dang!!! I
wasn't there to tell her a word about God. Heck . . . I
didn't know anything about God either. My family lost
the family Bible and no one in my parent's house went
to church either. We were lost and didn't know what
our problem was. We weren't let God operate in us at
all. That was a great mistake. I learned after Regina
had left home. It was too late, the devil had her.

Did you know that a child's life is greatly affected
by the type of love and affection that they receive

from people who are close to them? If love is scarce, a child is most likely to find love in a stranger or act out in a negative way, which draws negative attention upon him or her. Teaching a child the Holy Bible is an excellent way to teach them about love. The word Love is spoken about so many times in the Bible and it teaches us what it takes to really love others. It tells us that love is kind. Love is tender and desirable. Careful though, too much giving does not mean that is love. Too much giving can actually work against a parent. Children can expect more than they should receive. Well, that was not the case for my daughter, Regina. I didn't love her enough. I loved her, but I was so busy defending my feelings that I ignored her feelings. I needed love too. My parents didn't love me . . . so I found it in the street. Nope . . . I did not snort crack or shoot up heroin. My drug of choice was alcohol. I did my share of that and someone else's too. I had so many men coming in and out of my house that the neighbors thought I was a prostitute. I just had a lot of parties. Regina kept telling me that the men kept making passes at her, but I just ignored her.

One day one of my men friends tried to rape her and I caught him. I eat that man like he was a dirty rug.

Regina ran away from home and went to live with her best friend Helen. I thought that Helen was a nice girl until Regna called me and told me that she and Helen were lovers.

Regina told me that so that I would hurt inside. It worked . . .!.

Some people would find it hard to believe that I suddenly woke up to the fact that my daughter was a young lady now, even though she was only 20 years old. What I mean is I missed her growing up. I was sleep through her adolescence and her pre-teen years. I wasn't there for her. Right now, I am depressed as hell. I allowed her to raise herself. Regina needed a woman in her life so; she turned to her best friend Helen. I always thought that Helen was rougher than the boys, but I didn't think anything about it. The truth is; I feel responsible for her death. I don't know that boy was beating my baby. When I suspected it, Regina would always lie for him. Two times she went to the hospital. One time with a broken jaw and another time she said that she fell down the stairs and broke her arm.

The last time she went to the hospital she had internal injuries and I couldn't get her to stop talking. It was as if she was telling me that she didn't care about living any more. She started telling me about her relationship with Helen. I didn't know anything about my daughter. I cried so much that night. She said that Helen loved her the way that I never did. She was not talking about sex. She was talking about friendship and having someone to talk to. She spoke about the times that Helen would listen to her and try to understand her thinking. She said that when she went to the hospital the last time, Helen was there through it all . . . She also told me about the conversation they had the day before she went to the hospital when she told Helen that she wanted a boyfriend. She said Helen was emotionally hurt. Helen kept telling her that Bobby was a rough neck. Regina said that she like rough men. She felt like she had a father. Regina moved away from Helen and moved in with Bobby.

Bobby was the first man in Regina's life. You know how new love is. She didn't know how to pray to ask God to guide her in her decisions. She didn't have the experience to know that there were standards by which a decent man used when he loved his woman. Regina was lonelier than she was afraid. He filled her lonely heart but, he treated her like a dog! Regina kept asking her to leave this boy but, she was too scared to leave. Helen got her to come to church one day and she really liked it and wanted to go back. Bobby didn't want Regina to go to church because he thought she would make friends and they would talk her into leaving him. She kept going anyway. In the process, Helen got saved and turned away from homosexuality. Regina was doing real good and was about to be baptized, but one evening before bible study, Bobby staggered into the house and started yelling and screaming at Regina. He was accusing her of sneaking around with a man in the church. She got so nervous and scared because she could tell he was going to beat her up again. She was waiting for her mother to get there because she was going to ride to church with her this time. She finally talked her mother into coming to learn about God. This is what happened . . .

Regina
Bobby, don't do this. I have cooked your favorite meal today. Do you want me to warm it up for you right now? Do you feel like eating?

Bobby

You know you didn't cook, Regina. I don't smell a thing. What did you cook?

Regina

I did cook Bobby. It is in the oven, go look. Oh, well, if you don't want to eat, maybe you want to go to church with me and my mother.

Bobby

Hold on Regina, I am not messing with God and I don't want him messing with me! I know why you are going to that church. You got a man there, don't you?

Regina

No, Bobby! You are wrong. I don't look at any men in church. I am looking for the Lord. I want my life changed. Don't you want to change?

Bobby

Oh, so you are trying to change me now?

(He walks up on her and gets in her face)

Regina

Bobby, you are making me nervous. Don't do me like you did before. Don't do this, Bobby!

Bobby

I make you nervous? I make you nervous? I will show you nervous

(Bobby grabbed Regina by her throat and through her to the floor)

(Bobby started hitting and kicking her)
(Ruby entered)

Ruby
Regina, I came to bring you this dress for tonight

(Ruby saw Bobby beating Regina and lost her temper)

Bobby Davis!!! You get away from Regina. Boy I will kill you. Do you want to fight a woman, boy? Well, fight me. Come on, fight me. She has done nothing but be nice to your crazy behind.

Regina
Momma . . . let him alone. He is crazy. Ouch! . . . . o-o-o

Ruby
I'm calling the police

She was bleeding from her mouth and she said she had a bad head ache. I had a hard time keeping her alert. She kept falling to sleep

Regina was hurt real badly this time and she actually tried to protect him. She didn't want him arrested. In fact she wanted him to come to the hospital with us. Humph . . . I would have killed that child. Helen came to the hospital as soon as she heard about it. Regina died in her arms.

<u>Leola</u>

I am the most down to earth person that you would
ever want to meet. I don't cut corners when I have
something to say. If you don't want to know the truth
about something, don't ask Leola. Leola will not spare
your feelings. Yes, I am speaking in the third person,
because I want you to understand that it is my point
of view without a doubt. I am called Leola. That is
my name and I love me. I didn't always feel this way
about myself. There was a time that my self-esteem
was in the tank. Caution!!! If you are not at least 18
years old . . . stop reading RIGHT NOW! I'm grown
and I am about to talk about the birds and the bees
baby. Christians know the birds and the bees just like
you do (if you are not a Christian).

I was raped, like most women. Why is it so hard for
a man to contain himself? God did say "multiply"
and I know that men were built to have sex. They tell
me that a man think about sex every sixty seconds,
subconsciously. Whoa . . . I feel so sorry for them.
They wake up in the morning being reminded about
it and when they don't have a consenting woman in
their life, they are reminded of it more often than
they desire to remember. Sometimes, when they are
married to an unaccommodating woman, they feel the
heat too. A simple kiss, sometimes give them ideas.
That is a problem for most women. I am glad that I
am a Christian and I dress with caution because I am
less likely to have sexual abuse invade my life. A man
most often will think twice before approaching me in
that manner, if you know what I mean. Don't make a
mistake and think that Christian men are exempt from

this torture. They just pray a lot more. I would rather have a real Christian man than any other type of man because respect for God is in his heart. He would hesitate to anger God and therefore; he will do the right thing toward a woman (most times).

Anyway, I have desired and I enjoyed the experience we call sex, but I was taught about God when I was very young and I knew how to pray. In fact, I have prayed all of my life. I know that I haven't always lived the life of a Christian and it is a wonder that I am still alive to talk to you today. The problem with me was; I didn't believe in my belief. I said I believed, but my actions said otherwise. Ask me what happened to my belief. I will tell you. I couldn't find a Pastor who genuinely cared for my soul. I have been beautiful all of my life and my body . . . fine! Whatever . . . Many Pastors delivered sermons that she listened to and after church they broke their neck to get in my face to pass me their private telephone numbers. Humph . . . those hypocrites. I knew that God would deal with them at his own time. Sure to life, I would hear bad stories about each of them later on. My mother taught me a very important scripture when I was a very young and it came from Matthew 23:13. It reads "train them up in the way that they should go and when they are old, they will not depart from it".

I remember when she would lift me up from the floor, hug me tight and say it to me. I remember hearing my grandmother in the background yelling, "Hallelujah!" I had good Christian teachers in my life, but I got so confused watching the behavior of those who confessed

God. My Christianity had become dysfunctional and I had become paranoid about Pastors.

I find it a dishonor to God when leaders of the church have bad reputations and bad characteristics. I know that no one is perfect but, does it have to be so apparent? One more thing . . . why don't they ask for forgiveness at the altar? We do it. Can hypocrisy keep you out of heaven? I think it can because "thou shall not lie" is in the Ten Commandments and hypocrisy is nothing more than a lie that you live out loud. Secondly, these Pastors are not living the life they preach about. They give Christianity a bad name. They should stop this! I am sick and tired of these watered down and sugar coated messages coming from the pulpit. Say what the Lord tells us in the Holy Bible. Stop saying untrue things or words that sound good to sinners. Tell it like it is! It is easy. If you trust God, he will pay that church mortgage and those bills with new members who want truth. Stop selling souls short . . . stop it! One final thing that really irritates me is the leaders who do not have a spirit of discernment and/or carry a spirit of jealousy. "All are of filthy rags" in the sight of God and "All have sinned and have fallen short of the glory of God".

Yes, I am a child of the highest God and I just keep on keeping it real. Don't judge me . . . you might get judged. This is my story and I can tell it any way I want to. I can flip it, flop it or smack it clean . . .

*   *   *You will read about the life of Butch, Willie, Mary and the author in the upcoming book, "A Mother's choice". Stay tuned.

Dedication

My dedication of this work is to my sweet angels . . . my daughters. Two, who are still on his side with me and one who got very tired of being here and went on to that glorious place with my father. I dedicate this book to my Father, my mother, all of my grandchildren and my great grandchildren. I, last but not least, dedicate this book to my brothers and sisters who have gone to the other side and written about in this book.

A closing word from Rosie McGee

Thank you for your support of my work. It truly was a pleasure to write for you. I wish you an abundance of great health, extreme wealth and prosperity. Most of all I wish you love.